THE CHURCH LIBRARY HANDBOOK

THE CHURCH LIBRARY HANDBOOK

LaVose Newton

HARVEST HOUSE PUBLISHERS
Eugene, Oregon 97402

THE CHURCH LIBRARY HANDBOOK

Copyright © 1987 by Harvest House Publishers
Eugene, Oregon 97402

Library of Congress Catalog Card Number 86-080715
ISBN 0-89081-563-1

Printed in the United States of America.

CONTENTS

PURPOSE

1

Why a Church Library or Media Center?

CHURCH LIBRARIES ARE becoming an increasingly important part of the church program. Why? The Christian does not substitute Christian books for the reading of the Word, the Bible. Christian book-reading is supplementary; it clarifies, amplifies, and applies the truths of the Bible. This is why Christian leaders encourage Christian reading. Today "reading" includes "watching" and "listening" to the excellent Christian audio/visuals now available.

What Christian Reading Does FOR You:

Christian reading provides answers to your spiritual needs, whatever they may be. Through the variety of materials available, Christian reading: 1. explains how to become a Christian and how to grow as a Christian; 2. teaches and illustrates how to overcome temptation, how to know God's will for your life, etc.; 3. helps you to understand your Bible and your faith; 4. trains you for effective service for your Lord (witnessing, teaching, leading, etc.); 5. gives you living illustrations of the Christian life, faith action, and ministry; and 6. provides you with guides and materials for personal and family devotions.

Doesn't it appear that God has made special provision for these days of stress, temptation, and confused thinking?

What Christian Reading Does TO You:

"You become what you read" is an accepted truism and is an encouraging fact to the reader of good Christian books. Indeed, you find: 1. your mind expanding to take on the great thoughts and truths which you read, 2. your heart warmed with new faith and love for your Lord as you read of what He has done in and through other lives, 3. your will challenged to do the will of God, and 4. your spiritual eyes opened to see areas in your life, your personality, or disposition where something needs to be confessed and changed by God's power.

Nancy, a 10-year old, showed her mother a children's novel she had just read, saying, "I just asked Jesus to be my Savior like Mary did in this book." Twenty-two-year-old Lee asked Christ to be her Savior and Lord after reading of the peace and joy He gave a young woman in a novel she had read. As a result, she attended a Christian college and became a director of Christian education. George, a high school senior, gave his life to the Lord for full-time Christian service after reading a missionary biography.

Yes, you are changed by what you read, and if you are reading good Christian books you are probably being changed more and more into the likeness of your Lord.

What Christian Reading Does THROUGH You:

As your own understanding, faith, devotion, and love are deepened, this is reflected through your life to others. Your heart is enlarged to share your Lord; your testimony and service are more effective.

You will know of specific books to put into the hands of other people who have spiritual needs. These "printed ministers" can do for them what they have done for you.

A Church Library Offers Christian Education and Leadership Guidance and Training. The importance of each phase of church work demands informed and trained leadership. Yet many of our lay leaders face their tasks with little basic information and training. The church must help its workers by making available to them books and materials that will prepare them for effective service.

Even experienced or trained leaders realize a need for continued study and supplemental materials. No church is fulfilling its responsibility unless it provides an adequate library to meet the needs of all ages and all phases of Christian life and service!

A Church Library Provides Program Source Material. Youth leaders seek material for their expressional meetings, worship services, parties, projects, and clubs. Sunday school and Vacation Bible School leadership need additional story and worship materials, as well as craft and recreational helps. Teachers and devotional leaders require Bible-study aids, training helps, books on apologetics, illustrations, poems and inspirational readings, and witnessing techniques. High school and college students often need resource material in their studies. They also must find intelligent answers for questions and problems proposed by non-Christian professors and fellow students.

The church library is able to provide resource material to meet these needs.

A Church Library Enlarges the Church's Ministry. "Books are among the great ministers God has given to men," said James MacKay.

Christian literature brings the ministry of the church right into the home and the leisure hours. Good books and audio/visuals on Bible study, doctrine, inspiration, missions, and the example of Christian living (biography and fiction) extend the ministry many times beyond that which personal contact with the minister, teacher, or other leaders is able to do. It does not replace their ministry; it amplifies it.

Eyes have been opened, hearts melted, and life-changing decisions made over the pages of Christian books. The church must be eager to introduce its people to materials that will enrich their individual lives and, in turn, benefit the entire church and the cause of Christ.

A Church Library Replaces Inferior or Harmful Reading. Most children and youth will read, and there is much cheap and demoralizing material readily available to them. However, there is good news for those who care about the minds and hearts of the young. A large variety of Christian books with a fresh approach to the current interests and needs of children and youth is to be found in Christian bookstores today. The church must make these available in its library. Only an actual provision of and guidance toward interesting and challenging Christian books can encourage readers away from destructive reading toward that which builds Christian character and discipleship.

A Church Library Is More than Books—It's a Resource Center. The Church Library was once strictly a book library. Then some years ago we began adding flannelgraphs, pictures, flash cards, maps and charts, biblical objects, puppets, slides and filmstrips, missionary curios, and games. Now our concept has been expanded to include all the media that continues to be developed for us in the entire church program, as well as for the benefit of the individual church members.

Many church libraries now provide transparencies, cassettes, videotapes, video disks, compact disks (CD), computer software, and the equipment to play, use, or project them. These will increasingly become a high priority in our library inventory.

Cassettes and videotapes have a tremendous potential ministry—not only for church and home use, but in an extension program ministering to those people confined to their homes or in convalescent and retirement homes.

The value and ministries credited to the books in our libraries are now just as applicable to the visuals and listening materials. Therefore, our library manual will include all of these types of library offerings in Chapter 5. All library inventory will be referred to in the manual as "materials" or "items."

NOTE:
If you are beginning a church library or are in a very small church, do not let this expanded library picture frighten

or discourage you. No library begins with all, or even many, of these types of materials. They are pictures of growth and potential. You want to be aware of them, however, and be prepared to add any that your church library is able to handle as your program grows.

PREPARATION

2

How Do We Begin?

I F YOU WISH to have a library that is efficient, known to your entire church family, and used by them consistently—and of course you do—thorough preparation is essential. However, don't allow the details of the processing program or the potentials of the library picture to discourage you. Do what you can, as you can, and expect to grow, enjoying every moment.

Plan for Capable Handling

Enlist a library committee to oversee the program. If possible, select a representative of every age group and special interest group in the church. While this large representation is not required, it will promote interest in and use of your library throughout the church membership. Sell your committee on the many values of a church library and the expected benefits to the groups they represent.

One important advantage of a library committee, whether it is small or large, is that it assures the continuity of the library. Many libraries have fallen into disuse or have even been closed because of the death, moving, or retirement of the librarian. An active library committee shares in the concern for an ongoing library and will accept the responsibility for appointing a needed librarian replacement.

Committee Responsibilities

The committee is responsible to carry out the following:

1.   Select a librarian and at least two assistants. (The library leadership will grow as your library grows and as you add new types of materials.) Your librarian will probably become chairman of your committee. See two suggested library organizational charts on the following pages. The first organizational chart is very simple and is for a beginning or small library. The second chart is designed for a large library and is a picture of the form to which a library may grow. Use whichever applies to your current or anticipated beginning situation. Then let your library grow as your vision grows, and undergird it with a committee sufficient to help your vision become reality.

2.   Choose a location for the library.

3.   Determine the criteria for evaluating and selecting materials (books, visuals, audio/visuals, etc.) for the library. (Suggestions will be found in Chapter 3.)

4.   Select or approve materials for the library.

5.   Finance and obtain the library furnishings, equipment, and supplies.

6.   Determine the policies of the library. (Suggestions are included at the end of this chapter.)

7.   Plan the opening, advertising and use of the library, and its continual promotion. (See chapters 6 and 7.)

8.   Plan immediate and future ways of obtaining library materials. (See chapter 3.)

9.   Study the improvement of the library and its ministry.

10. Confer with and encourage the library staff. Hold regular meetings with the staff (quarterly will probably be sufficient).

LIBRARY ORGANIZATIONAL CHART
FOR A SMALL LIBRARY

Christian Education Board

Church Library Committee
Librarian, Chairman

Librarian
Responsible for obtaining library materials, promoting their use, and maintaining adequate library facilities, equipment, and supplies. Keeps financial records. Supervises assistants in all library activities.

Library Assistants
Process library materials, repair items, follow up on overdue items, circulate materials during library hours, and help maintain a clean and attractive library.

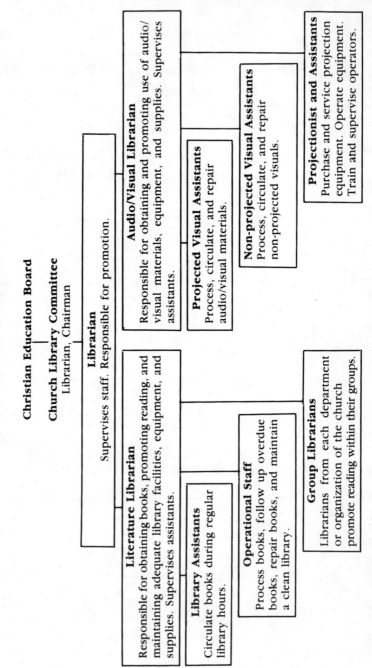

LIBRARY ORGANIZATIONAL CHART FOR A LARGE LIBRARY

Christian Education Board

Church Library Committee
Librarian, Chairman

Librarian
Supervises staff. Responsible for promotion.

Literature Librarian
Responsible for obtaining books, promoting reading, and maintaining adequate library facilities, equipment, and supplies. Supervises assistants.

Library Assistants
Circulate books during regular library hours.

Operational Staff
Process books, follow up overdue books, repair books, and maintain a clean library.

Group Librarians
Librarians from each department or organization of the church promote reading within their groups.

Audio/Visual Librarian
Responsible for obtaining and promoting use of audio/visual materials, equipment, and supplies. Supervises assistants.

Projected Visual Assistants
Process, circulate, and repair audio/visual materials.

Non-projected Visual Assistants
Process, circulate, and repair non-projected visuals.

Projectionist and Assistants
Purchase and service projection equipment. Operate equipment. Train and supervise operators.

11. Make regular library reports to the church board or Christian education board.

12. Pray for the library staff and the library ministry.

Someone may ask, "Is a library committee absolutely necessary?" No, it is not, but such a committee will greatly increase the effectiveness of your library.

The Librarian

Much of the secret of success or failure of your library rests in this person. The librarian and his or her asistants should be chosen carefully and prayerfully, keeping the following qualifications in mind.

1. Christian character, consecration, and cooperation
2. Appreciation of library materials and their ministry
3. Dependability, persistence, and patience
4. Love of detail
5. Typing ability (not essential, but very helpful)
6. Leadership ability—this is a real asset, though it may be supplemented through the committee.
7. Time to supervise processing of books and to keep library hours which suit the convenience of interested church groups. The assistants, however, share responsibility for these hours.

The Librarian and Staff

Duties of the librarian and library staff should include the following:

1. Pray for the operation and ministry of the church library.
2. Obtain approved materials for the library.
3. (Librarian) Supervise processing of materials and all mechanics of the library.
4. Keep up-to-date files and records on all library materials, finances, and activities.

5. Keep the library clean, neat, and attractive.
6. Frequently check shelves to correct any item misplacement.
7. Check all books before they are shelved for needed repairs. See that the repairs are made.
8. Post and maintain definite library hours.
9. Send overdue notices.
10. Discharge library materials and replace materials on shelves. Borrowers should not return items to shelves.
11. Meet regularly as a staff, the librarian assigning specific duties to each one.
12. Become familiar with the general content of the materials in the library.
13. Keep informed of new items which should be considered for the library.
14. Give courteous help in the locating of requested materials and offer interested counsel in their selection.
15. Inform library committee of problems or needs relative to the library.
16. Make book, visual, and audio/visual lists and other guides and encouragements for the various church groups and departments.
17. Periodically weed out items no longer desired, keeping a record of those discarded.
18. Constantly publicize the library. (See Chapter 7.)

Location

A separate room is essential for a good church library location and every library should aim for that. However, many cannot begin this way. Whether it be a quiet corner, shelves in the Sunday school office (not in the church office or other place which is busy during the week), a portable library on wheels, a converted closet or that much-to-be-desired room, the following must be considered:

1. Accessibility (ground floor, please, and close to

the church sanctuary, the Sunday school office, or other heavily trafficked area).

2. Attractiveness (cleanliness and color help to achieve this).
3. Size and number of shelves (for books—approximately 11'' high, 8''-10'' deep, with a support at every three feet of shelf length). Three feet of shelf will usually accommodate 25-30 books.
4. Good light and ventilation.
5. Adequate space for librarian's desk, supplies, and activities.
6. When your space permits, table and chairs for borrowers who browse or study.

Furnishings and Equipment

Choose your library furnishings and equipment in accordance with the size and nature of your quarters and the anticipated usage of the library. Endeavor to keep them consistent with your vision of the ministry of your library. The following are suggested for a full-service church library:

Bookshelves	Chairs
Cassette and videotape shelves	Card files
	Date file (charging
Shelves and/or cupboards for other visuals	tray)
	Reading table
Vertical file for certain visuals	Work table (folding table will do)
Cupboards for visual equipment & supplies	Dictionary stand
	Magazine rack
Floor covering	Bulletin board
Librarian's desk	Check-out desk

Library Policies

Before your library is opened, certain policies will need to be determined. The following should be included in your consideration:

1. What variety of library materials will you expect

to have in your library?

2. What will be the library hours? (One-half hour before and after every regular Sunday school or church meeting? Saturday mornings? From 4-5 P.M. on certain weekdays? Every weekday afternoon?)

3. What books are to be reference books (not removable from the library)?

4. Who may borrow materials from the library?

5. Will a "Borrower's Application" card be required for every user of your library? Or, will such be required only for children?

6. How many items may be borrowed by an individual at one time?

7. What will be the standard period of loan? (7 days? 14 days?)

8. Will renewals be permitted? For how long?

9. Will an overdue reminder be sent out when material is not returned on time?

10. Shall overdue fees be charged? If so, what will they be? (You might check with your public library and follow their plan.)

11. How will the fee money be used?

12. What about materials that are lost or ruined? Will you charge for them? If you do so, your accession list will give you the cost of any material purchased by the library.

13. How extensive a filing system is needed? Your library will grow; don't take shortcuts now that will require time-consuming changes later.

14. Should the library have permanent departmental or group branches?

Library Organization

Your library organization can be as simple as "one librarian" or "librarian and assistants." However, the more people involved in a responsible relationship to the library, the greater will be the interest in, concern for, and use of your library. So don't limit your library potential with low vision. Begin with as much leadership as you feel you can use effectively (and have available) and as your church size suggests. Your organization can grow as your library grows.

ACQUISITIONS

3

Acquiring Materials for Your Library

MATERIALS SHOULD NOT drift into your library! The dangerous temptation of many church libraries (particularly beginning ones) is to open its arms to all the materials that well-meaning friends discard from their personal libraries.

Because of its nature and purpose, the church library should be limited to those materials which minister to the spiritual, cultural, leadership training, and recreational needs of the church of which it is a part. A policy of accepting only those items which are on an approved list or which may be especially approved by the library committee will safeguard the library from outmoded, doctrinally or pedagogically unsound, or otherwise undesirable materials. This will also save the librarian the embarrassment of personally refusing unwanted materials.

Another important consideration in the choice of materials for your library is good subject coverage. There is a temptation to get heavy on pet subjects and to neglect some that would be of interest and value to many of your people. Try to have a fair representation in all classifications—for all ages, interests, and needs. Many subjects in classifications 250-265, of course, are more important to a minister's library than to a church library. Your church leadership or denomination may promote interest in certain subjects and your library will need to be well-represented in those areas. However, study the classification system (See page 95) and make sure your library includes the range of subjects important for Christian life, growth, and ministry.

Criteria for Selecting Materials

Here are suggested criteria for evaluating and selecting materials for your church library:

1. Does this material fulfill a need in our library?
2. Will it have a positive ministry to our people?
3. Is the doctrinal and moral content in accord with the teachings of the Bible and our church?
4. Are the facts reliable, authoritative, up-to-date, and presented by a person qualified in that particular field?
5. Is the subject matter presented in a fair and just manner?
6. Are the illustrations suitable for the text?
7. Has the material had favorable reviews?

One enthusiastic church librarian says, "When there is a choice between an expensive and a low-priced book, I have found that it is a good policy to purchase the higher-priced book for our library because our people often cannot buy it and will come to the library for it."

When books are available in both hardback and paperback, select the hardback for longer life and usefulness in your library.

Your library committee, minister, or denomination will probably suggest materials of special interest to your church. Christian magazines have helpful reviews. If you are beginning with a very limited book selection, choose a one-book Bible commentary and one, two, or three books from each of the following categories: Bible—general, doctrine, devotional, Christian home, inspiration for youth and adults, biography, Christian education, children's stories, and fiction for all ages.

Remember that a few newer and appealing books in your

library will be of more reading interest to your people than a larger number of old and perhaps outdated titles.

Maintain a Balance

To build a well-rounded library which will be usable by the whole church family, select a few books from each of the general headings in the classification system section of this manual. Select audio/visuals from as many classifications as are available. Try to maintain a balance among these divisions as you add to your library. However, you may find that the particular ministry of your church suggests emphasis in certain fields. Know the needs of your church and church family and build your library to meet them!

When a desired item for the library is brought to the attention of the librarian or member of the library committee, a *want card* (3 x 5) should be made on that item and put into a *want file*. Then when materials are to be added to the library, a selection is already prepared. When any of these items is obtained, its want card can be used as the work card (described later).

How to Obtain Library Materials

Churches are delighted to find that it is possible to build a good-sized library with a minimum of outlay from the church budget. However, every church and Sunday school should have enough concern for and appreciation of their library to write it into their budgets and thus assure the continual addition of new and needed materials. Here are suggested ways of consistently building your library:

1. *Library Materials Wanted!* Put a notice each month in your church bulletin or other publication that certain items (by type of material, title, author/artist/speaker and price) are wanted in the church library. Invite members to give one of the items listed. Such lists can also be distributed among adult Sunday school classes and organizations. Suggest that the money for the item, or the item itself, be given

to the librarian to avoid duplicate gifts.

2. **Birthday Gifts**. Promote the idea of each young person or adult honoring the Lord on his birthday, or the birthday of a friend, by bringing an item for the library on the Sunday following the birthday. Keep a list of desired materials, with prices, posted in each class that follows this plan. Adults have particularly responded to this program.

3. **Class or Group Projects**. A class may give the library a boost by contributing a certain number of new materials. Or, it may sponsor one phase of the library, possibly the section which would minister to its own members.

4. **Memorial Gifts**. A gift to the church library is a most fitting tribute or memorial for a Christian. It extends his testimony and ministry through the years. Library memorial funds are sometimes invited in lieu of flowers. Families may give a gift in memory of a loved one, or classes may so honor their deceased members. The memory of an outstanding leader in the church is beautifully honored through a memorial library in his or her name.

A memorial book, listing the names of those who have given library materials in memory of a specific leader, or someone dear to them, should be on display. It is a constant reminder of the memorial plan. Book name plates are available for different types of gifts—"In memory of_____," "In honor of_____," "Given by_____," etc. It may encourage gift-giving to place such a book plate in the front of each book given, allowing the donor to record the names on the name plate.

5. **Christian Bookstores**. The Christian bookstore is your best source of materials for your library. If you let them know of your interest and need, they will be glad to assist you with new book suggestions and books on consignment for a library promotion (Library Day, book fair, or book table, etc.). Many Christian bookstores offer a library discount with a substantial purchase. Let them be your library friend.

Library Day

You may say, "But we need lots of library materials right away. We're just starting our library," or "We don't have enough materials to interest people in coming to our library." Nothing so stimulates a church-wide giving of library materials and an immediate interest in using a library as a well-planned and publicized Library Day. In this plan, members of your church and Sunday school are invited to choose a book, visual, or audio/visual from among a select group of new materials on display and to give that item (the price of its purchase) to the church library. The next day the materials not purchased for the library are returned to the bookstore from which they were consigned, and those kept are paid for out of the money received.

The result? A good number of "just the materials you want" are ready to be added to your library without any cost to the church budget, and your people have seen or given materials they will want to read or use. If it is not possible to make a consignment arrangement with a local Christian bookstore, mimeograph a list of materials desired, with their prices, and distribute them to your members on your Library Day.

Many national, religious, or other special days give an opportunity for such a plan, such as Mother's Day, Father's Day, Children's Day, Memorial Day, Christmas, Christian Home Day, Thanksgiving, the day of the founding of your church, or the birthday of a beloved leader, such as your pastor.

For example, if Mother's Day is chosen, every member of the church and Sunday school is invited to give a book, a visual, or audio/visual to the library in honor of or in memory of his or her own mother. Many churches have placed 50 to 200 select items in their libraries by this Library Day method. It has proven so successful in some churches that they repeat it every year. They have built large, very active libraries in this way. Here is a suggested plan:

1. Assure the pastor's cooperation and confirm the date of your Library Day (Sunday is usually a good choice for

a Library Day). Set it a month or two in advance. Ask him to announce the project from the pulpit on two Sundays before the big day. On Library Sunday he might give a short challenge on the ministry of Christian reading, listening, and viewing. He should also explain the procedure to be followed after the morning service by all who wish to make a gift to the library. (The same program would be followed if your Library Day is held on Sunday night or on a weeknight.)

2. If your Library Day is held on a weeknight, make sure it will be a time which will bring out the majority of your church and Sunday school members. A church family dinner is an effective way to begin the evening. This is an excellent time for a challenge regarding the church library ministry and use. The library committee may even wish to put on a skit or to provide the evening's program. Your materials should be displayed in that same room, if possible, and directions given again as to the procedure for selecting and donating library material. Be sure that sufficient time is allowed for the people to look over the material displayed and to make their selection.

3. Announce the Library Day in your church bulletin and other publications for at least two weeks in advance.

4. Send out letters or cards to the church membrship, informing them of the new church library project and inviting them to give a gift from those displayed or listed in honor of someone special to them. Explain that their names will appear in the front of the books as donors, along with the names of those in whose honor the items are given.

5. Make announcements in each Sunday school department and church group of the forthcoming Library Day. Invite classes and groups to make group gifts. This stirs interest and encourages attendance at your Library Day.

6. Obtain book name plates (available at most Christian bookstores) on which is printed:

PRESENTED BY _____
IN HONOR OF _____
(or **IN MEMORY OF** _____)

7. Arrange with your local Christian bookstore to have a selection of desired materials to display in the church foyer or other convenient location on Library Day. Request that your pastor urge the people to go directly to the display tables as soon as the service or program is over.

Prepare tables to display the materials in such a way that your people may easily see and handle them. Arrange the books by subject matter, with an identifying easel-placard on each table. Also have a treasurer's table where each gift item is taken to be paid for and a book name plate signed and inserted in the book given. Provide library-addressed envelopes for those who want to give to the library. The gift items are stacked at one side, waiting to be checked with the receipts.

If mimeographed lists are used instead of an item display, each item chosen should be checked off a master list by the treasurer as he takes the money gift. This avoids duplication. A book name plate may be signed at this time for any book for which money is given, with the name of the book written at the top of the name plate.

Have borrower's cards ready for reserving "first-use rights" as soon as the items are processed for loaning. You may be surprised to see how many donors ask permission to be the first to check out and use their gift. Just what you want!

Return to the bookstore the materials which were not chosen as gifts, paying for the gift items from the money received. Or take the money and your master mimeograph list to your bookstore to purchase the materials chosen or to have them ordered for you.

CIRCULATION

4

Preparing Library Materials for Circulation

CORRECT AND COMPLETE cataloguing (processing) of each item that comes into your library is of extreme importance—beginning with the first item. Shortcuts are always regretted and take valuable time to undo and redo.

Using a Complete Classification System

A complete classification system is essential because it is elastic enough to allow your library to grow from a small project to a very large one without any change in the numbering or shelving arrangement. The purpose of the classification system is to allow all materials on a given subject and of the same type to be shelved together. No matter how many items are added to your library, each will be numbered and shelved in the right topical order and in right relationship to other similar materials on the same subject.

The classification system in this manual will assure this. It is the Dewey Decimal system, very slightly adapted for more convenient use in the church library program, and a bit expanded to allow for specific Christian interests. (This revised edition of the former *Church Library Handbook* adheres much more strictly to the Dewey Decimal system than former editions.)

Begin right! Then your displays will look attractive and your materials will be easy to locate and more frequently used. They will remain as permanent ministers in your library.

At first look, the classification system may appear cumbersome and difficult. However, as you see the general structure of it you will recognize a very natural and simple outline. The basic outline is according to broad subjects. Then those subjects are broken down into divisions or phases of that subject.

Your card files are very important and will answer such questions as—

> Where is *Design for Discipleship*?"
> Do we have any of Dobson's tapes?
> Have we a book on the subject of loneliness?
> Who has "Improving Your Serve"? When will it
> be returned?
> Have my high school teachers used this trans-
> parency?
> How many of our books are out on loan?
> How many videotapes do we now have in our
> library?
> How many transparencies have we added to our
> library this year?

These any many other important questions relative to the normal functioning of a good library suggest a careful, routine treatment of each item which comes into your church library.

SUPPLIES NEEDED

Adequate supplies and equipment should be gathered before preparation of materials begins. (See the Appendix for samples of the supplies marked with an asterisk.) The following is a recommended list:

> * 1. Book pocket (one for each book and for
>   some visuals)

 * 2. Date due slips (one for each book)
 * 3. Book cards or borrower's cards (one for each item)
   4. Work cards (one for each item)—not essential, but very helpful
   5. Title cards (one for each item)
   6. Author cards (one for each item). These include speaker, artist, etc.
   7. Subject cards (one for each item that involves a subject; some items may involve more than one subject)
   8. Book name plates (one for each donated book)—not essential, but recommended.
   9. Overdue reminder cards or forms
*10. Shelf classification labels
*11. Window stencil
  12. Classification system (see this section in the manual)
*13. Accession book
*14. Financial record
  15. Alphabet file card guides (for 3 x 5 cards)
  16. Card file(s) to hold 3 x 5 cards
  17. Date file, or charging tray
  18. Borrower's file
  19. Paste (vegetable glue or a library paste are recomended)
  20. Wide felt-tipped marking pen for making black score background for classification number on book cover or jacket or pressure-sensitive white labels to place on book cover or jacket (3/4").
  21. White ink and pen for writing classification number on black score or black nylon-tip pen (such as Pentel) for writing number on white label.
  22. Clear plastic book jacket covers or roll of clear plastic to be fitted onto book jackets.
  23. Clear plastic tape (3" x 4" wide) for paperback books

24. Rubber stamp with name and address of
    your church library
25. Ink pad
26. Typewriter with good ribbon
27. Dating stamp—not essential, but convenient
28. Book repair kit

Your local Christian bookstore may have many of these
supplies, or they can get them for you. If not, library
houses will serve you. See page 53 for names and ad-
dresses.

PROCESSING BOOKS

Correctly processing books for your library is a gratifying
project as you contemplate its far-reaching ministry. A well-
directed and equipped crew of workers will consider this
project an interesting and challenging experience. Form an
assembly line and the work will move quickly and smoothly.
The more people helping to establish and operate your
library, the more interest and enthusiasm will be stirred
toward its use.

Accession Each Book

Record the book on your book accession list (separate
accession lists are needed for each type of material) and give
it an accession number. A loose-leaf notebook, with dividers separating the different types of materials being accessioned, is recommended. Accession sheets and binders are
available from Christian bookstores or library supply houses.
Or you can produce your own sheets, using as a sample the
one shown in the Appendix of this manual. The first book
placed in your church library will be accessioned as number 1, and each book thereafter will receive the next number
in chronological order. Write this accession number on the
title page of the book, just above the name of the publisher,
and in the upper right hand corner of the back of the book
jacket. *Note*: this is not the classification number, nor the
one by which you shelve your book.

Classify Book

Classify each book with a classification number (also called "call" number)—the number by which you will shelve your book. The classifying system given in this manual is the Dewey Decimal system, very slightly adapted for more convenient use in the church library. (See the "Classification System" Section). In this listing, all subjects (except 020 and 030) are treated only as they relate to Religion, Christianity, the Christian life, ministry, doctrine, or the Bible. This sometimes results in a different classification than the usual Dewey Decimal System, but it simplifies the system for the church library and makes a more convenient arrangement for church library users.

Study the system first so that you understand its general plan. Then determine the classification number of your book and write this number in the top left corner of the title page in the book. Under this number write the first three letters of the author's surname, capitalizing just the first letter (Lewis—Lew). With books on individual biography, use the first three letters of the individual's name rather than that of the author.

The "Church Library Subject Listings" Section will be a further aid to you in determining the classification number of a book.

Large-Print Books

Large-print books will be classified like regular-print books. However, they will have an "L" above the classification number:

L
248.4
Cow

and they will be shelved together. Large-print Bibles will also have the "L" above the number and will be shelved with the large-print books.

Fiction and Children's Books

Fiction and children's books will need only their letter

classification, plus the first three letters of the author's last name. See the end of the classification system for these classification letters. All procssing procedures should be followed. Subject cards, however, are not needed.

Reference Books

Reference books, such as commentaries and dictionaries, are usually restricted to use within the library. If this is your policy, write a large "R" in front of the classification number in these books. The "R" will also be used this way on the book jacket and on each card. These books will not need book pockets, borrower's cards, nor date-due slips.

Pamphlets

Many pamphlets are important additions to your library. Process them just as you do the books, typing "Pam" above the classification number on the file cards and the borrower's cards. If you put your pamphlets into cardboard bindings, they may be shelved in their regular places among the books. A pressure-sensitive label should be on the front cover at the left edge and same height as on a book, with the same information as is put on the spine of a book. Be sure to put "Pam" above the classification number.

If you group your pamphlets, filing them in pamphlet boxes (available from library houses), write your inclusive numbers (example: 242-249) on the long end of the box, just as you do on a book, and shelve them in a separate pamphlet section. Small pamphlets could be housed in your vertical files.

Magazines and Periodicals

Your library undoubtedly will subscribe to certain Christian and educational periodicals. Stamp each issue with your library name. These need not be accessioned or classified, but they should be recorded on a file card. Make one card for each periodical, listing on it the issues as they are added to the library.

This card should have the periodical title at the top. Down two spaces, and beginnning two spaces from the left margin, type the year of the magazine issue, a dash, and the month. Each time a new issue comes into the library, add that month to that year line. (Example: 1986—March, April, May). After several years, when a card is full, begin a new card and clip it on top of the old one. File periodical cards alphabetically and in a group by themselves, perhaps at the back of your title card file.

Care and Treatment of Books

Press open all new books. Taking time to open new books properly will preserve their bindings. Place back edge of the book firmly on a table. Turn the front cover down until it touches the table, finger-pressing the edge where the cover joins the body of the book. Do the same with the back cover. Then turn down several pages at a time, alternating from front to back, until you reach the center and the book lies flat when open.

Use a dull-edged knife to separate pages that have not been cut apart.

Clean soiled books with an art eraser. Repair torn pages or covers with the materials from your book repair kit. Do not use substitute items, such as cellulose tape, for book repair.

Book Covers

Book jackets are designed to stimulate reading interest, so it is wise to keep them on the books. Increasing numbers of church libraries are covering their book jackets with a plastic cover, in this way protecting but displaying the colorful book jacket. The added cost is well compensated for by the increased life of the book. Plastic covers come in various sizes and can be obtained from some Christian bookstores or from a library supply house. Since quantity prices are more reasonable, two or more church libraries buying their plastic covers together will earn helpful savings.

A less expensive way to cover a book jacket is to buy a

roll of medium-weight clear plastic (available from a fabric or lumber store). In this case, the plastic is cut to fit each book, allowing one extra inch on all sides of the jacket. The extra edges are folded over and taped to the jacket with clear magic tape. The jacket is then taped to the book.

Another fine way to protect jackets is to apply a clear adhesive plastic, such as Contact. This material includes its own directions. Or, you may simply cover the spine of the jacket with a clear plastic tape (approximately 4'' wide), allowing the plastic to reach 1'' to 2'' onto the front and back of the jacket. It is always wise to cover paperback books either with the adhesive plastic over the entire cover, or the plastic tape over the spine as descibed above.

Cards and Files

1. *Work card* (or shelf card). If the person classifying the books does not type or have a typewriter accessible, or if he or she will not be preparing the book and file cards, it will be particularly important for that person to prepare a work card (3 x 5) from which all other cards will be typed. This can be handwritten. However, this work card will prove valuable to any librarian as a "shelf card," giving her information regarding every card on each book in the library. This card also proves helpful in removing all cards on a book that is being permanently removed from the library.

```
                    Screwtape Letters
     242        Lewis, C. S.
     Lew
                Macmillan        c1943

 Subjects: TEMPTATION
           SATAN
           ANGELS
```

Sample work card

Below the information arranged like a title card, the various subject card headings are listed in capital letters. Put the work card inside the front cover of the book, awaiting further processing. Shelf cards are filed separately and are used only by the librarians. They are filed numerically by their cataloguing classification numbers.

2. *Title card*. Type the title of the book two spaces from the top of the card and 12 spaces from the left margin. Drop down two lines and begin the classification number two spaces in from the left margin. Ten spaces from the left margin, type the author's name (surname, comma, and given name or initials). Author's name is always on the same line as the classification number.

Screwtape Letters

242   Lewis, C. S.
Lew

Sample title card

If you do not keep a work card in your files, you need to type the subject headings (for which subject cards are being made) half-way down on the title card. See illustration on work card. If the book should ever be permanently removed from the library, all the cards on that book can also be removed from the files.

2. *Author card*. Two spaces from the top, type the classification number and the author's name (surname, comma, and given name or initials). Start the classification number two spaces from the left margin, the author, ten spaces from the same left margin.

Drop down two more lines and, beginning 12 spaces from the left margin, type the book title. Two more spaces down and ten spaces from the left margin, type the name of the publisher and the copyright date. Place a small "c" in front of the date.

```
242          Lewis, C. W.
Lew
                    Screwtape Letters

             Macmillan      c1943
```

Sample author card

If no author is given for the book, type in its place the name of the editor, compiler, or publisher (in that order of preference). If a book has more than one author, prepare author cards for each of the first two authors named.

The classification number and author always appear on the same line.

4. *Subject card.* The subject card, to be filed alphabetically according to subject, helps your readers to locate a book on some subject which may or may not be indicated in the title. The content of some books may suggest several subjects, each requiring a separate subject card. (See the "Church Library Subject Listing" section for suggestions.)

The subject card is typed just like the author card except that the subject is put on the top line two spaces from the top of the card and 12 spaces from the left margin), and the author and title lines are each correspondingly dropped two spaces. The subject is typed in all capital letters.

```
                    TEMPTATION

242          Lewis, C. S.
Lew

                    Screwtape Letters
```

Sample subject card

Filing Your Cards

If you have a small library, you may wish to file all of your cards in one file. You can either alphabetize them together or separate the title, author, and subject cards, alphabetizing them within each type of card. The latter method is preferred. In a larger library, or as your library grows, you will want to file each type of card in a separate file.

There are some general rules for alphabetizing which you may wish to follow. Alphabetize according to the first word ("In preparation" comes before "Information"). Disregard any beginning articles (The, An, A, etc.). Consider abbreviations and numerals as if they were spelled out. Mc and Mac are filed like Mac. Most hyphenated words are considered one word.

Computers are being used in many church libraries today. They are great time-saving aids in setting up or expanding the files for your library. You can set up your word-processing program or data-base management system to store the information on your library books, visuals, and audiovisuals. When a library file card "program" is set up on a computer, it is necessary to type the card information on each item only once. then the computer will type each of the four kinds of cards on pressure-sensitive labels which you will press onto your 3 x 5 file cards. Pressure-sensitive labels (1-7/16"x 4"), in strips or on a roll, are usually available from your local office supply store.

It may be helpful to print a letter code on each type of card (T—Title, A—Author, S—Subject, SH—Shelf) being prepared. Type this in the bottom right-hand corner of the label.

It generally takes one to two hours (depending on computer experience) to set up your program. From then on it requires only one to two minutes to enter each individual item.

Or, if you have a minicomputer in your library, you may wish to put your library material completely on the computer—to be read from the computer, rather than making file cards by computer.

Borrower's Card

5. The Borrower's card (book or pocket card—See sample in the Appendix.) is a preprinted card which can be obtained from your Chrisitan bookstore or library supply house. The author's name and book title should be typed on the lines specified. Type the classification number in the upper left corner and the accession number in the upper right corner.

This is the important little card which locates loaned books. It is kept in the book pocket in the book while it is in the library. When the book is loaned out, the card is removed from the pocket, the borrower's name and the due date (date by which the book is due back in the library) are written on it, and it is filed in a "Date file" according to the date it is due back in the library.

The Date file should have two month dividers ("This month" and "Next month"), 31 date dividers, and 1 "Overdue" divider. "This month" divider will have behind it the date dividers from the current date through the end of the month. "Next month" will have behind it the dates from the first up to the current date. For example, on May 14 the order of the date file will be as follows: This month, 14-31; Next month, 1-13; Overdue. These should be changed each day the librarian is on duty.

A borrower's card should also be made on periodicals, clipping each card to the first inside page, for a record of their loan. Shelve your periodicals on slanted shelves, if possible, and in stacks, each title in a separate stack, always keeping the latest issue on top.

Further Procedures

1. Stamp the name of your church library, including the name of your church, on the title page, just beneath the publisher's name.

2. If the book was a gift to the library, paste a name plate on the inside front cover (or on the page facing it), first filling in the name of person or organization giving the book and the name of the person in whose honor it was given.

3. Paste the book pocket below the center on the inside of the back cover. If you are using plastic covers on your book jackets, paste the book pocket on the page opposite the inside back cover. Write the accession number in the upper right corner and the classification number in the upper left corner of the pocket. Now place the borrower's card in the pocket.

4. Paste the date due slip (See sample in the Appendix) on the page opposite the book pocket. In paperback books, or books where this page has printed material important to the reader, paste the date due slip on the book pocket just below the classification number.

5. Print the classification number and the first three letters of the author's name on a pressure-sensitive label, using a black nylon-tip pen. Draw a line 3/4'' from the bottom of the book or book jacket spine. This will serve as the lower edge of your label. An even white or black strip across your row of books is important to an attactive library. Now attach the label to the spine of the book or book jacket, placing it so the lower edge of the label rests on the drawn line.

Another method of labeling your books is to draw a black score 1'' high and beginning 3/4'' above the bottom edge of the book or book jacket spine. To be sure the blank scores are the same size and distance from the bottom of the book, use the window stencil found in the Appendix of this manual. Making sure the bottom of the stencil is even with the bottom of the book or jacket, pencil in the top and bottom margins of the stencil. (Marks-A-Lot works well in drawing in the black score.) Now print the classification number on the score with pen and white ink or with an electric pencil and white transfer tape. The electric pencil is easier to use and results in neater and clearer writing.

Paperbacks should be processed exactly like the hardbacks. If the spine of the book is not wide enough to take the classification number clearly, place the label or stencil the black score (at the regular height), beginnning at the left edge of the front cover to an inch wide. Shelve them with the hardbacks.

6. If you have not already covered the book jacket with some type of plastic covering, as described earlier, now is the time to do it. With paperback books, it is always advisable to either cover the entire book with a clear Contact-type of plastic or to apply the plastic tape to the spine. Your paperback books will hold together much longer than normal.

7. Your work card can now be filed in a "shelf card file."

Shelving Your Books

Shelve your books numerically according to their classification numbers. Where you have two or more books with the same number, shelve them alphabetically by author (note three letters under the number). When you have two or more books with the same number and the same author, shelve them alphabetically by title.

Large-print books and Bibles will be shelved together, following the last numerical classification (290.3). Within their section they will be shelved by their classification numbers. The first large-print book on your shelves might be:

L
213
Mor

Fiction for adult/youth (F) may be shelved following the large-print books and Bibles, followed by T (young teens). Fiction and children's books will need only their letter classification, with the first three letters of the author's name beneath. See the end of the classification system for these classifying letters.

All children's books should be located on separate shelves and within a child's easy reach. A special children's area is always a delight in a library. These books should be shelved according to their letter classifications (B.C.E.Fc, and J), with the first three letters of the author's name beneath.

If you have foreign language books in your church library, you may want to shelve them between the large-print books and the adult/youth fiction. If you have a large number of foreign language books, it might be wise to shelve them completely separate from the English language books.

Label the shelves according to subject matter so that your books in each grouping may be easily identified. A set of 30 subject classification labels is provided in this manual for this purpose. These labels can be taped, stapled, or tacked to the shelves, or they will readily slip into metal shelf label holders such as are used by public and school libraries. These are available in many Christian bookstores.

Post your library rules, "How to Use Your Library," in a conspicious place in your library. Suggested rules will be found in the supplies section of this manual. If you have a lettering artist in your church, ask this friend to letter the rules on a poster large enough to be read from a little distance.

Library Supply Houses

Brodart—P.O. Box 3137, Williamsport, PA 17705
Gaylord Bros., Inc.—Box 4901, Syracuse NY 13221-4901

VISUALS AND
AUDIO/VISUALS

5

Visuals and Audio/Visuals

T HE PRODUCTION AND USE of visuals and audio/
visuals, in a widening variety, is a rapidly growing
and much-valued enhancement to the entire Christian
ministry. Cassettes and videotapes are gradually covering
most subjects and types of presentations that books now
do. They are available for evangelization, inspiration,
instruction, and recreation. They appeal to all ages and
interests. They extend the ministry into the home, hospi-
tal, retirement centers, nurseries, schools, and out around
the world. They often minister where books cannot. So it
is understandable that what was once considered a luxury
is now acknowledged as a necessity to an effective church
program. Therefore our procurement, care, and circulation
of these materials is very important.

Some churches have a separate audio/visual library. Most,
however, seem to feel that visuals and audio/visuals are a
part of the total library program and they house them
in the church library or church media center. Whatever
arrangement you may have or wish to have, certain procedures will be important to good maintenance and use of
your visuals and audio/visuals. These will vary with the
different types of items, and suggestions will be made for
several types. Whether or not you use all of the suggestions
will probably depend somewhat on the size of your library

57

or the number of your non-book items. You must choose. But if you have any anticipation of or vision for an expanding library of visuals and audio/visuals, it will be of great benefit for you to follow specific procedures from the very beginning—either these being suggested or others you may prefer.

Every visual and audio/visual should be accessioned, classified, and have a file card or cards, a borrower's card, and a book pocket (if possible). Each type of visual has a separate accession list. Accession sheets for visuals are available, as well as book accession sheets. These are loose-leaf sheets that fit into a special binder available from library supply houses. However, you can produce your own sheets, using as samples those shown in the Appendix of this manual. Each accession list uses a type code and should begin with number 1 (e.g. "VC-1" for the first videotape acquired). This accession number, including the code letters, will always be placed in the top right corner of the borrower's card, the file card or cards, and the visual or audio/visual. The classification number will be in the top left corner. The classification number should have the visual type name (videotape, picture, transparency, etc.) above the number wherever it is used. Each visual should also have your church name and library identified somewhere on it. The type code and variations in processing will be explained with each type of visual or audio/visual.

Audio/Visual Borrower's Card Files

Two audio/visual borrower's card files will need to be kept at the check-out desk. Many of your non-book items cannot have a borrower's card with them and such cards will need to be in file number one (borrower's card file). When such an item is to be borrowed, it is taken to the librarian who removes the card from file number one, has it dated and signed by the borrower, and files it in file number two (date file). When the item is returned, the card will be pulled from file number two and returned to file number one. The date file will have numbered dividers (1-31) and "This Month" and "Next Month" dividers. If your current date is October 5, your arrangement of dividers would be "This Month" 5-31, "Next Month" 1-4. When an item is borrowed, the borrower's card will be placed in front of date "19" (the date 2 weeks from the current date—the date when the item is due back in the library).

Your borrower's card file may have a divider for each type of visual or audio/visual you have in your library, although in a small library one "Visual Date File" will do. The cards will be filed alphabetically within those type dividers. If your number of non-book items is very limited, you may be able to keep your date file at the back of file number one (borrower's file).

Date due slips are not feasible for most visuals and audio-visuals. In lieu of these, you can attach a small pressure-sensitive tape to the item being borrowed, on which you would write the appropriate due date.

Audio/Visual Requisition Form

It is always advisable to have audio/visuals and their required equipment reserved ahead of the time needed so as to avoid disappointment if the desired material is already in use or has been spoken for. For this purpose you may want to prepare a requisition form. Here is a sample form which can be duplicated and made available to your audiovisual users.

AUDIO/VISUAL LIBRARY REQUISITION

Type of Audio/Visual desired:_____

Name of Audio/Visual desired:_____

Organization to be served:_____Date needed:_____

Location where the Audio/Visual will be used:_____

Operator in charge: _____

Please furnish an Operator: Yes _____ No _____

Please furnish Equipment: Yes _____ No _____

Material will be picked up _____—or—Please deliver the
   material _____

Request is made by: _____Date: _____

_____ Church Library

PROCESSING NON-PROJECTED VISUALS

Non-projected visuals (charts, graphs, flannelgraphs, flash cards, games, maps, models, objects, pictures, puppets, etc.) are often kept in the departments in which they are used. However, if they are maintained in the church library they will be available to all of the teachers and leaders in the church. Your arrangement needs to please those most involved. If they are kept in the church library, each visual should be accessioned, classified, and have a borrower's card, a pocket (if the visual has a place for one), and a file card. If it is not possible or wise to attach a pocket or borrower's card to the visual, keep a separate file for the visual borrower's cards (as described above) and write or clip the name of the visual, the classification number, and the accession number onto the visual.

```
Flannelgraph                          FL-6
226.9
            Sermon on the Mount


```

Sample borrower's card for visuals

The following code letters may be used with the accession numbers for non-projected visuals:

Charts and graphs	CH	Models	MOD
Flannelgraph	FL	Objects	OBJ
Flash cards	FC	Pictures	PIC
Games	GMS	Puppets	PUP
Maps	MAP		

Many of the non-projected visuals (charts, graphs, pictures

flannelgraphs, flash cards, small maps, etc.) will be housed in a vertical file, such as a steel file. These should be kept by individual story in their original folder, a manila envelope, or a three-tab manila folder, putting the classification number (including type of visual) and title on the side of the folder (see sample above).

The borrower's card can be kept in a pocket pasted inside the file folder. For protection of the materials when such a visual is borrowed, the desired material should be placed in a manila envelope (if it is not already filed in one). The borrower's card is also removed from the folder and kept in the date file until the visual is returned.

Although cassette tapes and compact disks are non-projected visuals, their treatment is so similar to the projected visuals that we will discuss their processing and shelving with the projected visuals.

Some of your non-projected visuals (games, models, objects, puppets, etc.) can be shelved best in a cupboard. Open shelves can be used.

PROCESSING PROJECTED VISUALS AND AUDIO/VISUALS

Some projected visuals and audio/visuals will be a natural part of your library immediately. Others listed may not find their way into your library for some time, if ever. Don't let the list confuse or trouble you. If you are sensitive to the interests and needs of your people, when any audio/visual becomes important to your library, you will know it and then you can use the information given.

Projected visuals and audio/visuals should be accessioned (with type code), classified, and have borrowers' and file cards. They will need title and subject cards; author cards are needed only where an author or artist/group is named. If your library is using all white or buff cards for your title, author and subject cards, you may wish to use a colored card for your projected or audio file cards. This will easily identify them, particularly if they are filed with the book file cards. The following visual code letters are suggested. These may be used with the accession number:

Compact Disks	CD	Computer Software	CS
Cassette Tapes	CT	Filmstrips	FS
Microfiche	MF	Microforms	MF
Motion Picture Films	FI	Multimedia Kits	K
Records	RE	Reel-to-Reel Tapes	TA
Slides	SL	Transparencies	SL
Video Disks	VD	Videotapes/Cassettes	VC

Because audio/visuals are often a part of home libraries, it is easy to lose a church visual in a home library unless each is clearly identified. Therefore, it is important to put the name of your library, including the name of your church, on each audio/visual, as shown on the example below.

Slides and Filmstrips

Slides and filmstrips may be stored in their original containers (boxes and cans), with the classification number, title, and accession number (including type code) typed on a pressure-sensitive label and attached to the box or can. Borrowers' cards will need to be kept in the visual borrower's file (at the check-out desk) and moved to the date file when the item is borrowed.

```
Filmstrip                                          FS-3
226.9          Sermon on the Mount
               Central Bible Church Library
```

Sample filmstrip container label

Filing Transparencies and Records

Transparencies and records can be filed in a vertical file

in their original envelope or in a manila folder. The pocket can be attached to the envelope or inside of the folder.

Filing Microfiche and Computer Software

Microfiche, microforms, computer software, etc. should each be placed in a separate envelope with the classification number, title, and accession number typed across the top of the envelope. The borrower's card can be kept in the envelope and moved to a date file when the item is borrowed.

Videotapes

Videotapes (Videocassettes) are of two types—Beta and VHS. Each type requires a player/recorder made for that type. Most videotapes for the Christian market are VHS, so, if your library is going to get a videotape player/recorder for loan, it is wise to obtain a VHS player/recorder.

Videotapes, cassette tapes, and compact disks (non-projected) can be identified with a narrow pressure-sensitive tape attached to the edge of the cassette box which is visible when shelved or filed. On the tape will be printed the title, author/speaker/artist, the classification number, and the accession number (both with their code letters). Borrowers' cards will need to be kept in a separate file. When one of these is borrowed, the borrower's card will be moved from the borrowers' file to a date file. In a small projected-visual library, the date file can be at the back of the borrowers' file, with dated dividers. These audio/visuals can be filed on shallow shelves (1/4" to 1/2" higher than the visuals).

It is possible to make a jacket for each videotape or cassette tape by cutting a stiff poster board to a size 1" longer than the tape height and 2" wider than twice the tape width. Then fold it around the tape to fit like a jacket. Paste a pocket on the inside back of the jacket. Write the classification number (with the visual type), the title and the speaker or artist on the spine of the poster board jacket. This should also be recorded on the front of the jacket, along with the name of your church library. It is also wise to place this same information on one side of the tape. Paste a second pocket on the inside front of the jacket, placing a borrower's card in that pocket. These can then be shelved like books. (See illustration below.)

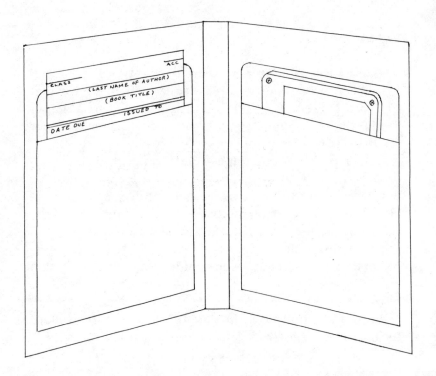

Sample tape jacket

At least one church library keeps the tapes in drawers (made to size), with coded dividers between tapes. Borrowers' cards are inserted in front of the tapes.

When you have a series of tapes on one book of the Bible (often the case with pastors' sermons), follow the classifying number with a dash and the chapter and/or verses covered.

Audio/Visual Equipment

Audio/visual equipment, called "hardware" (projectors, tape recorders, videotape player/recorders, compact disk players, etc.) will undoubtedly become part of the provision of the church library that develops a good audiovisual department. These will require special care and probably should be locked in a cupboard and used only by someone trained in their use and care.

Using Computers in the Church Library Program

The computer is another visual that is fast becoming part of the church library program. Whether you have your own microcomputer in your library or are hooked up to your church's computer or an outside computer by phone, the computer will do many valuable services for both the library staff and users. It can replace card files with easy access to all types of listings, statistics, and important information on your library inventory, available materials, usage, etc. More and more library services will become available to computer users in the days to come.

PROMOTION

6

Open Your Library with a Flourish!

MAKE YOUR LIBRARY Grand Opening an event which will entice every prospective library user in your church to visit "their" new library. This event can be on a weeknight, a Sunday morning after church service, Sunday afternoon before the evening service, following the evening service, or a combination of times. Whatever time is chosen, a dedication of the church library should be a part of the morning service the day of the opening or the Sunday preceding a weeknight opening. The librarians and library committee members might be called to the front of the church for a dedicatory prayer.

Planning Your Library Grand Opening

Set your date far enough in advance to assure the completion of shelving procedures and the decorating of your library. Appoint a publicity committee to plan the event and to arouse the interest and curiosity of the entire church family. This committee should be a part of, or work with, the library committee. Place an announcement in your church bulletin for at least two weeks before the event. It is also helpful to have written and verbal invitations sent to every church home and organization. Eye-catching posters could be displayed throughout the church. Headings might include the following ideas:

- Come and meet the newest member of our church staff—the Church Library!
- Don't be an odd-ball! Be a part of the latest and best—our new Church Library!
- Miss Church Library will make her debut...DON'T MISS IT!
- Come and see your answer to prayer...
- What will you tell your friends—if you miss the Grand Opening?

Program Ideas

1. *Book fashion show.* Members model book jackets as the moderator describes the book—its contents, ministry, etc. Represent one book each out of several sections of your library. Jackets can be made of poster board in a true three-dimensional rectangle, or the front and back boards can be stapled to burlap pieces which cover the shoulders and act as side seams. Wide butcher paper may also be used for front and back covers. Sketchy reproductions of the jacket of each book being modeled can be painted and lettered.

2. *Cassette and videotape fashion show,* playing or showing a short part of one or two tapes as the model walks around. The model, of course, should be "wearing" a tape.

3. *Storybook displays,* reading interest centers, audio and visual displays, floral decorations, and a tea table with light refreshments will add interest.

4. *A bookmark,* listing the library hours and the types of material available for loan, will make a nice little gift for each visitor and will serve as a reminder to return to the library.

5. *Book reviews* by an outstanding speaker or reviewer.

The books reviewed should be among those in your library.

6. *Short play or skit* on the practical value of Christian reading, viewing, or listening in the home.

7. *Short lecture* on the influence of the printed page, with a challenge to replace harmful or inconsequential secular reading with a personal program of Christian reading.

8. *Personal testimonies* on what Christian materials have done for individuals.

9. *An announcement party*, announcing the birth of the church library, or the marriage of your church to Miss Christian Material (and "let not man put asunder").

10. *Formal dedication*, with music by the choir or choir members, including a ritual with charge and acceptance of usage responsibility repeated by pastor and people. Golden keys to each of the library sections, or library subject sections, could be given to leaders of the Sunday school and various church organizations. Or ribbons attached to these sections (or attached to posters representing the sections) might be given the leaders who would stand while the charge and dedicatory prayer are given by the pastor. Some visible way of relating each group in the church to your library is effective.

"Visit the Library" Time

A good way to encourage the children and young people of your church to use your church library is to arrange a "Visit the Library" time with each department of your Sunday school. Schedule each visit for the beginning or ending of their class period. This can be done over a period of months after your library opens. The plan can also be repeated every few years. During these visits you would show the classes where materials of interest to them are shelved. Explain how they can check out materials, how many they can take out at one time, and how long they may be kept out. If you are using membership cards, explain and distribute the applications at that time. For children under 12 years old, it is wise to have a parent's signature on the application. Assure them of their welcome in the church library and encourage their reading of, listening to, and viewing of Christian materials.

Checking Out Material

Someone wants to check out a book, a visual, or a tape? This is what you have been preparing for! When the borrower has selected his item, he removes the borrower's card from the pocket or the item, signs his name on it, and takes both card and item to the librarian. The librarian stamps the due date (date when the item is due back in the library) on the date due slip and on the borrower's card, which she keeps as a record of the loan. It is filed in the date file. If there is no borrower's card evident (some cards for visuals must be filed separately), the librarian will locate the card and, after it is signed and dated, will file it in the date file.

The date file should be checked weekly and reminder notices sent, or phone calls made, regarding items overdue more than seven days. When an overdue item is returned, if an overdue fee is charged, the librarian might say, "I see you are investing 40 cents (or amount of fee) in new material for the library." Take the sting out of your fees, but be consistent in charging them if they are a part of your library policy.

The librarian may wish a record of the borrower's name, address, and phone number. This is especially helpful when your borrowers are children—and you do want a lot of them. You may want to provide library membership cards for the children.

7

Promote! Promote! Promote!

"SOMETHING AS FREE as a library still must be sold." In spite of the tremendous ministry possible through a church library, an unused or neglected library is worthless—a heartbreak! The publicity chairman on the library committee should employ every possible means of keeping your church "library-minded"! The following are suggested ways to continue publicizing your library.

The Best Publicity—An Enthusiastic User

First, let me say that the very best publicity is an enthusiastic user. Personal testimonies from people who have been blessed by a particular book or other library item (or even the consistent use of the church library) does more to awaken interest and activity than any other type of promotion. Encourage Sunday school departments or classes and adult organizations to invite enthusiastic readers or listeners to tell of the effect some book or tape has had in his/her life.

Announcements in Church Publications

Place frequent or regular announcements in the church bulletin and other church publications. At least once a

month include a list of "New Materials in Our Library."
Occasionally insert an article about the influence of reading upon children and youth. Urge parents to check out
books for their children as well as for themselves.

Recommendations from the Pulpit

Encourage your pastor to recommend books and other
materials in your library from the pulpit. Librarians whose
pastors do this have instant demand for those items and
others like them. When you know the subject of your pastor's sermon on any given Sunday, bring a library item or
two to him before the service (earlier, if possible) and ask
if he would like to recommend them to the congregation.
He may appreciate this encouragement.

Compile Special Reading Lists

Special reading lists could include the following:

    a) lists geared to age or group interests and sent
       to these groups (children, youth, church
       leaders, Sunday school workers, missionary
       society, etc.).
    b) basic Christian home reading list given to all
       church members. Make out a new one each
       year.
    c) same list and an invitation to use the church
       library sent to each new church member.
    d) list of books pertaining to marriage and the
       Christian home (including daily devotional
       helps) sent to each newly married couple in
       your church. e) list of books pertaining to
       parenting in the Christian home sent to the
       parents of newborn babies in your church.

You may wish to extend your ministry by sending such
a list, with an invitation to use your church library, to
parents of newborn babies in your community—or to newly
married couples.

Audio/visual lists can be separate or included with the

reading lists and used the same way.

New-Item Reviews

Short new-item reviews can appear in your church publications, also in various departments or groups to be read or given in person by the librarian or library representative.

Book Reviews

Book reviews by children, young people, or adults in their own departments or group programs. These have proven exceptionally effective wherever used.

Invite people to review specific books or other materials from your library and to report to you. If their report is worthy, ask permission to post it on a poster, bulletin board, in the church bulletin, etc. Or ask the reviewer to give the review in a Sunday school department or church group.

Posters

Library posters in Sunday school departments and other conspicuous places around the church. Have poster contests for different age groups. This will not only provide you with posters to move between departments or areas of the church, but it will undoubtedly enthuse the poster makers with the library. They will have contributed to it!

Make a poster for each age group, with a picture of one of their reading members at the top. Use a caption such as "This book is great!" "I liked this book," "This was fun reading," "You should hear this!" "This tape really touched me," "This book brought blessing to our home," "This book set me thinking," etc. A picture or drawing of the item which the person is recommending can be pasted to the poster below the caption.

Bulletin Board

Make a library bulletin board in the library and also in

departmental rooms. Post reading, listening, and viewing lists here. Lists of new items should be posted regularly.

If you have an artist in your church, solicit his or her talent in reproducing the covers of new materials you want to promote. A short, interesting review, or a statement of the item's particular ministry, should be alongside of the cover picture. A snapshot of one of your readers/listeners, with a short testimony of what some material has meant in his or her life, will get good attention.

Reading Contests

Hold reading campaigns or contests, awarding prizes to the department or persons reading the highest number of pages from books in your church library. Summer is an excellent time for a reading campaign among children and youth.

Reading contests can be built along the theme of travel, space, missions, sports, etc. Rules for youth and adult contestants might include a requirement of reading one biography and one inspirational book in each four books read for credit.

Extra credit may be given to each contestant who influences someone else (a friend or member of his family who does not attend your church) to read a book from your library.

Book Club

Start a book club, requiring the reading of just one book a month (more, if you wish). Book club membership could be posted in the library, with competition among departments or church groups for the largest number of book club members.

Family Reading Club

List names of families who regularly "read as a family or as a couple" at the table, before going to bed, or other selected times.

Story Hour

Start a story hour on Saturday mornings, a weekday afternoon, or as a Sunday school pre-session activity. Tapes can also be used for this purpose.

Appoint Group Librarians

Group librarians appointed by each Sunday school department and church group can bring appropriate books and tapes from the library to their rooms each Sunday morning or meeting day. Cooperating with the head librarian, these group librarians may check items in and out, returning the signed borrowers' cards and the unloaned items to the library at the close of each meeting. Women's associations, mothers' clubs, men's groups, youth organizations, and Sunday school departments can greatly encourage and increase Christian reading and listening through their group librarians. Here are some hints for group librarians:

> a. Send Bible story and other books with a definite Christian message home with children from non-church homes.
> b. Place Bible story and child psychology books and tapes on tables by parents' chairs in preschool departments. Post a sign inviting parents to examine them and to check one out to take home.
> c. All parents' groups should have books and tapes at their meetings which will help them understand and influence their children for Christ.
> d. Give or arrange for special reviews in Sunday school classes or adult meetings of books or tapes for the Christian home, with a word about their ministry and how they can be used in the home. give reviews of books and tapes for children and youth in their departments.

Workers' Conference Librarian

The workers' conference librarian will come to each

meeting of the Sunday school teachers and officers well-supplied with books and tapes on teacher training and teaching helps. During the departmental meeting time he or she can go from department to department with just those items which are important to leaders of that age. This is an effective way of assuring the continual study and growth of Sunday school workers. One church developed well-trained teachers in this way.

Library Skits

Put on library skits in Sunday school and church group meetings. A large "cardboard book" might walk into a meeting and tell its story—complain of loneliness or ill-treatment, tell excitedly about the fascinating things to be found in its pages, talk about the interesting or funny people who have recently read it, relate what happened in the life of one who read it, etc.

LIBRARY WEEK

Library Week is a national endeavor to develop or encourage the habit of reading—good reading! It is an accepted fact that reading influences and directs thinking, feeling, belief, desire, and action. This being true, we as Christians are concerned with this same endeavor—with a Christian purpose. We want a Christian reading program, one which will influence hearts and minds (our own, other Christians' and those needing Christ) for God.

Strange as it may seem, many Christians are not familiar with Christian books and audiovisuals; others do not know where or how to obtain them, and still others do not realize the relationship between Christian reading and Christian growth and fruitfulness. Library Week is the concerned leaders' opportunity to inform, awaken, and stimulate them to Christian reading. We should encourage every member of our Sunday school and church to develop the habit of reading, watching, and listening to Christian materials for instruction, inspiration, and pure enjoyment. How can we do this? An active church library is our obvious answer!

The Church Library as a Ministry

If you have an adequate church library you have the tools for a varied and far reaching spiritual ministry thoughout your church family and community. "Adequate" means that you have materials covering every age group and every subject of Christian concern (Bible study, doctrine, apologetics, evangelism, discipleship, missions, Christian marriage, Christian home, Christian parenting, inspiration, devotions, social problems, leadership training, program materials, biography, fiction, recreation, youth challenges, and children's books).

Maybe your library needs the addition of some new materials to make it of current interest or to meet areas of need now neglected. This would be an excellent time to enlarge. Other needs should also be made known (new or impoved fixtures, better of larger location, more staff, etc.). Reports on the usage, growth, and benefits of your church library should be presented this week.

If you have no church library as yet, this could be the time to start one. Or even better, set up or enlarge your library early enough to be able to promote the using of Christian materials during Library Week.

Assuming you have a church library, or will have one in time to promote it during Library Week, how can this week be used to advantage in your church program? Advance preparation is the secret of a successful Library Week. Here are some suggestions.

Advance Preparation for Library Week

1. The library committee plans programs, publicity, and goals. If you do not already have group representatives, appoint a library representative in each department and group in your church to aid in carrying out the Library Week program in his or her own group.

2. Library Week posters made for every Sunday school department. (Attractive library poster sets are available from your Christian bookstore.) A poster-making contest would

stimulate interest among your young people.

3. Publicity written in all of your church and organizational publications.

4. A reading contest can be started or completed during Library Week. Only books from your church library or other Christian books will count for reading points. You might wish to require a balanced reading program, such as one book from each of the following: Bible study book or book about the Bible; inspirational or devotional book; missionary or biographical book; miscellaneous book (fiction, Christian home, leadership training, etc.). The requirements will vary with different ages.

Each book must be reported, giving the title and number of pages. Readers enlisting outsiders in the contest should be given extra credit. This is library evangelism.

5. Do any redecorating, furnishing, or other improving needed to make your library inviting and interesting.

6. Displays. Each department or organization is invited to prepare a display visualizing the value of Christian reading. A prize can be offered for the best display.

7. "My Reading Experience." Mimeograph a reading questionnaire to be given to the congregation on Library Week Sunday. This might include such questions as:

> How many books have you read this calendar year (approximately)?
> How many of these have been Christian books?
> What has been the effect of Christian reading upon your life this year?
> What do you consider to be some of your needs which might be met by reading Christian books?
> Believing in the ministry of Christian reading, how many books (average per month) do you propose to read during the remainder of this year?
> What types of books (or on what subject) do you wish to read?

Will you advance the ministry of Christian books by encouraging others (Christians and non-Christians alike) to read books which have helped you or which you believe would be of help to them?

NOTE: This questionnaire is intended as a personal challenge to the reader or potential reader and is not to be seen by anyone else.

8. Suggested reading, listening, and viewing lists, prepared from among your library materials for various ages and interests. These can be given out in Sunday school or church on Library Week Sunday, or could be mailed to your church and Sunday school families with a letter telling about Library Week at your church.

Library Week Sunday in Your Church Service

The cooperation of your pastor during the church service will bring the ministry of the church library before many prospective library users. Some pastors have directed their sermons to such topics as "Books and The Book in Your Life," "You Are What You Read," "Who directs Your Thinking?" Others have used a portion of the service for a short message on such a topic.

The pastor may commend the church library and its ministry and urge his people to participate in the entire Library Week program of their church. The Library Week schedule, printed in the bulletin, can be reviewed.

This is a particularly appropriate time for the church librarian to be introduced in the pulpit and given an opportunity to invite the congregation and famillies to visit and use their church library. Library hours should be mentioned.

Library Week Program

A weekday program may be an alternative to Library Sunday or may be scheduled in addition to the special Sunday. Here are some possible activities.

1. *Monday night "Family Reading or Listening/Viewing Night at Home."* Some families might read a book together, such as a Christian biography, or listen to a tape and/or view a videotape together. Others, because of their age or interest difference, may want to read individually. Parents could read first to their very young children, then do adult reading or listening when the children are in bed. A suggested reading list will be of help here. Make much of the reading fellowship evening; maybe it will become a habit!

2. *Midweek prayer meeting.* Particularly pray for the ministry of your church library and for all of the library personnel. Ask God to enlarge its outreach and to convince your people of the importance of Christian reading, listening, and viewing, and to meet any needs of your library.

3. *Friday night "Library Wonder Night."* This is a family night at the church which should be packed with fun and thrill. Everything done that evening should have originated in your library—games, stunts, program and devotions. During the evening several people might be called upon (by prearrangement) to tell of some "wonder" which they have discovered in their library (an interesting fact of archaeology, of Bible background or study, or an unusually challenging thought regarding the Christian life, etc.) These statements should be only one to three minutes each.

A helpful and interesting presentation would be a short demonstration of "How Our Family Uses Our Church Library" or "How the Church Library Ministers to Our Home" by a family actively using Christian materials.

The feature of the evening might be "The wonder of a Story," a 20-30 minute story told by an experienced story-teller. This could be a missionary adventure, a biography, etc.

Close your evening with a short devotional read from one of the devotional books in your library . . . and with refreshments, of course!

4. *Saturday "story hour" for children of primary or junior ages.* A one-hour program could include a few songs, a half-hour story by the "Story Lady," and a hand-puppet presentation of some Christian truth suggested in the story. The puppet might discuss the story a bit, relate it to a Scripture verse, and apply it to the children's lives. Cookies and punch could be served.

Quotable Quotes to Use in Promotional Materials

"If religious books are not circulated widely among the masses in this country, and the people do not become religious, I do not know what is to become of us as a nation.

"And the thought is one to cause solemn reflection on the part of every patriot and Christian. If truth be not diffused, error will; if God and His Word are not known and received, the devil and his works will gain ascendancy; if the evangelical volume does not reach every hamlet, the pages of a corrupt and licentious literature will; if the power of the Gospel is not felt through the length and breadth of the land, anarchy and misrule, degradation and misery, corruption and darkness, will reign without mitigation or end."

—Daniel Webster

"No man can be truly educated or successful in life unless he is a reader of books."

—Benjamin Franklin

"A truly great book teaches me better than to read it. I must soon lay it down, and commence living on its hint . . . what I began by reading, I must finish by acting."

—Thoreau

"Reading Christians are growing Christians. When Christians cease to read, they cease to grow."

—John Wesley

"Good books on shelves won't make us wise, won't train, inspire or catechize. But those we read, absorb, apply will surely Christian growth supply."

"Good reading does for the mind what good glasses do for your eyes; it lets you in on the details of living."

Your Library Is a Trust

If it were possible to keep a record of decisions made and lives blessed and changed as a result of using the materials from your church library, you would have an exciting book—a bestseller!

Keep your library growing and your vision growing! Make the library current with and related to the interests, needs, purposes, and programs of your church at all times.

The library is one of the valuable ministries of your church. Like any other minister, however, it must have access to your heart and life it it is to be effective. Pray for it! Support it! Use it!

PERSONAL
LIBRARIES

8

Building a Home Library

A HOME LIBRARY is a special treasure and joy to those of us who love books. To have choice reading at hand for reference, for review, for personal enjoyment, as well as for sharing, is a privilege we do not take lightly.

Many of the book-processing procedures used by the church library are not necessary for a home library, but a few are helpful in locating desired books and in keeping track of those loaned to friends. If you would like to make your home library of maximum benefit, you may want to consider the following:

1. Paste a book name plate in the front of each book, with your name written on it. Or, have a stamp made which might read, "From the library of _____. Please return."

2. Classify each book according to the classification system included in this manual—just like the library does. Print this number and the first three letters of the author's name on a pressure-sensitive label which you will attach to the spine of the book (for a paperback) or to the spine of the book jacket. To assure an attractive shelf, let the bottom of the label be one inch above the bottom of the book.

3. Shelve these books numerically according to the clas-sification number.

4. If you do not wish to classify your books, shelve them first according to subject matter (Bible reference books, Christian life, marriage and Christian home, biography, fic-tion, youth interest, children's books, etc.), and then by author within each subject area.

5. Prepare books for loaning. There are several ways to do this—here are three suggestions: a) Make a borrower's card (book card) for each book you will be willing to loan (see chapter 4 for instructions) and place the card in the book like a book mark. When the book is borrowed, remove the card and record on it the date and name of the borrower. Keep these cards in a little box on your library shelf. When a borrowed book is returned, replace its card in the book. b) Use a "borrower's check book" which has perforated bookmarks to be torn out and placed in any book being loaned. Your name is written on the bookmark. The bor-rower's name, along with the title of the book and the date, is recorded on the stub in the checkbook. These are handy and are available at most Christian bookstores. Keep a "shar-ing" notebook in which you record the name of the book, the date, and the name of the borrower. When the book is returned, cross out the information recorded.

Types of Books to Include in a Home Library

Whether or not you use any of the above procedures, you will undoubtedly want to have a well-balanced library, with books to meet the needs of your entire family and to sup-plement and encourage your ministry to others. Here is a list of some types of books you may wish to have in your library (according to your family interest and need):

Bibles (various   Daily devotions
   versions)   Christian life and
Bible atlas   character
Concordance   Books for men

Bible dictionary
Commentaries
Other reference books
  such as a Bible hand-
  book, Bible customs,
  Introduction to the
  Old Testament or to
  the New Testament
Apologetics (Evidences
  of Christianity)
Special studies such as
  the Tabernacle,
  Feasts, etc.
Doctrine
Prophecy
Evangelism

Books for women
Christian biography
Marriage and the home
Parenting
Books on health
Children's Bible stories
Children's Christian
  character stories
Children's Christian
  fiction
Teen-age fiction
Youth inspiration and
  relationships
Youth and adult fiction
Discipleship
Prayer

Whatever you have in your home library, make sure that reading is an important activity in your home. One Christian leader advised, "Always be into a Christian biography." Good advice! Encourage family members to share their enjoyment of books at the table and during other family gatherings. Display your reading interests by leaving your books on your coffee table, bedside table—even in the bathroom. Read, talk, and share books. Let your friends and neighbors know that you like to share your blessings.

9

The Minister's Library

A MINISTER'S LIBRARY is a most essential tool of his ministry and therefore should be arranged in such a way as to make it easy for him to find desired information. It is usually large and, while heavy in reference works, includes a wide range of subjects. Because of this it is most helpful to give each book a classification number and shelve the book by that number. This assures that books on any given subject will be shelved together and easy to locate. The regular process of writing the classification number (with the first three letters of the author's name below) on a pressure-sensitive sticker and placing it on the spine of the book jacket should be followed. (See chapter 4 and the "Classification System" and "Church Library Subject Listings" sections in this manual.)

Subject Card File

A subject card file will also be an invaluable aid to the minister. In this file he can quickly locate every book in his library that treats any subject he may wish to study. This is particularly helpful with books that treat a variety of subjects, such as books of sermons, books on the Christian life, etc.

Putting the minister's library listing on computer will

make the information even more readily available to that busy person.

Many ministers and Christian leaders have also put their clipping/article files on the Dewey classification system. Each manila folder is numbered (classification number) for the type of material that is to be filed in it. Again, this is a great convenience to the person either filing materials or looking for materials on a given subject. Sermons can also be classified this way. It is wise to write the classification number in the top left corner of the material being filed so that, when it is removed for study, it is easy to replace it in the correct folder. It is also important to write the date and source of each clipping or article in the top right corner of the material to be filed.

CLASSIFICATION SYSTEM

CLASSIFICATION SYSTEM

000   **GENERAL WORKS**
      020   Library Science
      030   General Cyclopedias and
                   Dictionaries
      050   General Periodicals

200   **RELIGION**
      205   Periodicals, Magazine
      207.1   Christian Schools
      208   Religion in the World Today

213   **CREATION—CREATION VERSUS
              EVOLUTION**

215   **SCIENCE AND RELIGION**

220   **BIBLE**
      220   Introduction, Study and Teaching
      220.1   Origins and Authenticity
      220.12   Canon
      220.13   Inspiration
      220.14   Authorship
      220.15   Prophecy (See 236 for prophecy of
                   "last days")

220.2   Bible Handbooks
220.3   Dictionaries, Encyclopedias
220.4   Concordances, Topical Text Books
220.41   Original Texts, Manuscripts
220.5   Bible Versions
220.53   Bibles in Other Languages
220.6   Interpretation or Criticism
220.7   Commentaries
220.71   Bible Questions or Problems
220.8   Special Topics (Music, Games,
              Animals, Plants)
220.9   Bible Geography, Chronology and
              History, Atlases, Bible Lands in
              Bible Times, Customs
220.92   Scriptural Biography
220.93   Antiquities, Archaeology
220.94   Bible Studies and Courses—
              General
220.941   Bible Studies and Courses—
              Old Testament
220.942   Bible Studies and Courses—
              New Testament
220.943   Home Bible Study Classes and
              Studies (see 254.51)
220.944   Special Studies (Tabernacle, Feasts,
              etc.)
220.9505   Bible Stories—Youth and Adult

221   **OLD TESTAMENT**
221   Texts, Introduction
221.62   Chronology, Geography, and
              History
221.7   Commentaries or Studies on Old
              Testament

222   **LAW AND HISTORICAL BOOKS**
222.1   Pentateuch
222.11   Genesis
222.12   Exodus
222.13   Leviticus
222.14   Numbers

222.15	Deuteronomy
222.2	Joshua
222.32	Judges
222.35	Ruth
222.43	1 Samuel
222.44	2 Samuel
222.53	1 Kings
222.54	2 Kings
222.63	1 Chronicles
222.64	2 Chronicles
222.7	Ezra
222.8	Nehemiah
222.9	Esther

223   POETICAL BOOKS

223.1	Job
223.2	Psalms
223.7	Proverbs
223.8	Ecclesiastes
223.9	Song of Solomon

224   PROPHETS

224	Major Prophets
224.1	Isaiah
224.2	Jeremiah
224.3	Lamentations
224.4	Ezekiel
224.5	Daniel
224.6	Hosea
224.7	Joel
224.8	Amos
224.9	Minor Prophets
224.91	Obadiah
224.92	Jonah
224.93	Micah
224.94	Nahum
224.95	Habakkuk
224.96	Zephaniah
224.97	Haggai
224.98	Zechariah
224.99	Malachi

225   **NEW TESTAMENT**
225.09   Geography, History, and
                Chronology
225.1   Introduction
225.3   New Testament Dictionaries and
                Encyclopedias
225.4   New Testament Concordances
225.7   Commentaries and Studies on the
                New Testament

226   **GOSPELS AND ACTS**
226.1   Harmonies
226.2   Matthew
226.3   Mark
226.4   Luke
226.5   John
226.6   Acts
226.7   Miracles
226.8   Parables
226.9   Sermon on the Mount
226.93   Beatitudes
226.96   Lord's Prayer

227   **EPISTLES**
227.1   Romans
227.2   1 Corinthians
227.3   2 Corinthians
227.4   Galatians
227.5   Ephesians
227.6   Philippians
227.7   Colossians
227.81   1 Thessalonians
227.82   2 Thessalonians
227.83   1 Timothy
227.84   2 Timothy
227.85   Titus
227.86   Philemon
227.87   Hebrews
227.91   James
227.92   1 Peter

227.93	2 Peter
227.94	1 John
227.95	2 John
227.96	3 John
227.97	Jude

228   REVELATION

229   APOCRYPHA

230   DOCTRINE—THEOLOGY

230.042	Catholic Theology
230.044	Protestant Theology (all varieties)
230.1	Doctrines of Specific Denominations and Sects

231   GOD (General Topics and Concepts) AND TRINITY

231.1	God the Father
231.2	God the Son
231.3	God the Holy Spirit
231.72	Kingdom of God
231.73	Miracles
231.765	Creation (or see 213)

232   CHRISTOLOGY (Life of Christ)

232.1	Incarnation, Messiahship, Typology
232.2	Christ as Logos (Word of god)
232.4	Cross, Atonement, Sacrifice, Passion
232.5	Resurection (Jesus)
232.6	Second Coming of Christ
232.8	Divine Humanity and Diety
232.9	Family and Life of Jesus
232.954	Teachings of Jesus

233   MAN—CREATION, FALL, SIN

234   SALVATION AND GRACE

234	Faith, Redemption, Eternal Life,

242.101	Devotions for Pre-teens (Juniors)
242.11	Devotions for Young Teens
242.12	Devotions for Youth
242.2	Devotions for Adults
242.21	Devotions for Specific Classes of People
242.23	Devotions for the Family
242.24	Christmas Observances and Meditations for the Family
242.25	Easter and Lent Observances and Meditations for the Family
242.4	Prayers and Meditations for Times of Illness, Trouble and Bereavement
242.8	Collections of Prayers
242.9	Poetry and Readings

243   **EVANGELISTIC WRITINGS (For Individuals and Families)**

248   **CHRISTIAN EXPERIENCE, PRACTICE, AND LIFE**

248.29	Charismatic Experience and Practice
248.3	Worship
248.32	Prayer
248.34	Meditation
248.4	Christian Life and Practice
248.41	Comfort (In Problems, Illness, and Death)
248.411	Christian Leadership and Management
248.412	Christian Stewardship and Financial Management
248.42	Christian Marriage
248.421	Divorce and/or Remarriage
248.422	Interfaith Marriage or Mixed Marriage

248.43   Christian Home and Family
            (Including Family Activities)
248.432   Parent-Child Relationship
248.433   The Exceptional child or
            Handicapped Child
248.434   Single Parenting
248.435   Sex Education
248.436   Home Education
248.44   Singles
248.5   Witnessing, Personal
            Evangelism, Discipling
248.83   Youth Inspiration
248.842   Christian Man
248.843   Christian Woman
248.844   Hospitality
248.845   Nutrition and Health
248.846   Cookbooks
248.85   Aging and the Senior Years,
            Retirement

250   **CHRISTIAN CHURCH**
250   Institutions and Work

251   **PREACHING (Homiletics)**
251.01   Preparation
251.02   Sermon Outlines
251.03   Delivery
251.08   Illustrations

252   **SERMONS**
252.1   For Specific Occasions (Baptisms,
            Confirmations, Weddings,
            Funerals)
252.3   Evangelistic
252.53   For Children
252.55   For Youth
252.56   For Senior Citizens and Those
            Experiencing Illness, Trouble,
            and Bereavement
252.61   Advent and Christmas

252.62	Lent and Holy Week
252.63	Easter
252.67	Other Feast and Fast Days
252.68	Secular Occasions (Thanksgiving)
252.7	Consecrations, Ordinations, and Installations
252.9	Memorial Occasions

253   PASTORAL DUTIES

253.2	Life and Person (Including Pastor's Wife)
253.3	Marriage, Funerals, and Baptisms
253.5	Counseling and Psychology (Including Lay Counseling)
253.7	Conversion, Evangelism, Soul Winning, and Discipling

254   CHURCH GOVERNMENT AND ADMINISTRATION

254.3	Use of Communications Media
254.4	Publicity and Public Relations
254.5	Membership
254.51	Lay Leadership, Development, and Ministry
254.52	Home Bible Classes (See 220.943)
254.6	Programs and Organizations
254.7	Building, Equipment, and Grounds
254.8	Finances

259   CHURCH ACTIVITIES WITH SPECIAL GROUPS

259.3	Senior Citizens
259.4	Handicapped and Ill
259.6	Bereaved

261.1   CHURCH AND SOCIETY

261.11	Christian Ethics
261.5	Christianity and Secular Disciplines

(Philosophy, Psychology, Technology, Art, Literature, Education)

261.7   Christianity and Political Affairs

261.72   Religious Freedom

261.8   CHRISTIANITY AND SOCIAL PROBLEMS

261.83   Social Problems (Abortion, Drug Abuse, New Morality, Racism, Rock Music)

261.831   Child Abuse, Wife/Husband Abuse, Parent Abuse

261.832   Alchoholism

261.833   Crime

261.835   Relation of the Sexes (Including Homosexuality)

261.836   Ecology

261.86   Poverty and Starvation

261.87   International Affairs (Including War and Peace)

262.1   GOVERNING LEADERS OF THE CHURCH

262.9   CHURCH LAW AND DISCIPLINE

263   DAYS, TIMES, PLACES OF RELIGIOUS OBSERVANCE

263.9   Christmas, Easter, Pentecost, Lent

263.91   Thanksgiving and Other Non-religious Days

264   CHURCH WORSHIP AND LITURGIES

264.2   Music

264.21   Hymnals, Songbooks

265   SACRAMENTS AND ORDINANCES

265.1   Baptism

265.2   Confirmation

265.3   Holy Communion (Lord's Supper)

265.5   Matrimony

265.8   Ministry to the Sick and the Dead

266   **MISSIONS, GENERAL; MISSIONS AND THE SUNDAY SCHOOL**

266.022	Home Missions
266.023	Foreign Missions
266.0231	Asia
266.0232	Africa
266.0233	Europe
266.0234	South America
266.0235	North America
266.0236	Central America
266.0237	Miscellaneous Countries
266.025	Medical Missions
266.09	Missionary Stories

267   **BIOGRAPHY**

267.1	Missionary Biography, Individual
267.2	Missionary Biography, Collective
267.3	General Biography, Individual
267.4	General Biography, Collective

267.9   **ORGANIZATIONS FOR CHRISTIAN WORK**

268   **CHRISTIAN EDUCATION, General**

268.1	Administration
268.11	Evangelism
268.2	Buildings and Equipment
268.3	Personnel
268.4	Teaching Methods and Teacher Training
268.401	Age Psychology
268.402	Teaching the exceptional or Handicapped
268.403	Teaching the Blind
268.41	Teaching Aids, Visual Aids
268.42	Audio/visual Aids
268.421	Object Lessons
268.422	Quiz Books
268.423	Programs (Graduation, Promotion)

268.432   **CHILDREN'S DIVISION**

268.4321	Cradle Roll

268.4322   Nursery
268.4323   Kindergarten or Beginner
268.4324   Primary
268.4325   Junior
268.4326   Children's Sermons and Story
             Material

268.433 **YOUTH DIVISION**
268.4331   Junior High or Intermediate
268.4332   High School
268.4333   Youth Materials (Other than
             Sunday school)

268.434 **ADULT DIVISION (Including College age)**
268.435   Extension or Home Department

268.47   **WEEKDAY ACTIVITIES**
268.471   Vacation Bible School
268.472   Weekday Church School, Child
             Evangelism Classes
268.473   Clubs (Bible and Other)
268.474   Craft, Handwork
268.475   Drama, Costumes
268.476   Plays, Pageants, Programs
268.477   Recreation, Parties, Games,
             Puzzles, and Camping
268.477H   Humor
268.478   Etiquette
268.479   Miscellaneous: Nature Study, Flags,
             and Patriotism

268.5   **RECORDS AND RULES**

268.6   **SUNDAY SCHOOL CURRICULUM**

269   **SPIRITUAL RENEWAL (Revival)**

270   **CHURCH HISTORY**

280   **DENOMINATIONS AND SECTS OF THE
         CHRISTIAN CHURCH (See 250)**

290	**OTHER RELIGIONS**
290.1	Judaism
290.2	Cults and Isms
290.3	Ideologies (Humanism, Existentialism, tialism, Rationalism, Socialism, Fascism and Communism)

B	Bible Stories for Children
C	Character Building Stories for Children
E	Easy Reading for Children
F	Fiction for Youth and Adults
Fc	Fiction for Children
J	Fiction for Juniors or Pre-teens
T	Fiction for Young Teens
L	Large-Print Books and Bibles
O	Foreign Language Books and Bibles

CHURCH LIBRARY SUBJECT LISTINGS

CHURCH LIBRARY SUBJECT LISTINGS

A

Abortion	261.83
Abstinence	248.4
Abuse (Child, Parent, Wife, or Husband)	261.831
Acts	226.6
Activities for Senior Citizens	259.3
Administration, Christian Education or Sunday School	268.1
Administration, Church	254
Adolescence	268.4332
Adult Division, Christian Education	268.434
Adult Fiction	F
Advent	263
Advent Meditations	242.24
Africa, Missions in	266.32
Age Psychology	268.401
Aging	248.85
Agnosticism	290.3
Alcoholism	261.832
Allegories	226.8 or F,J,T,Y
Amish	280
Amos	224.8

Amusements	261.11 or 268.477
Ancestor Worship	290
Anecdotes	H or 251.08
Angels	235.3
Animals	220.8
Annuals	254.4
Anti-Communist Efforts	290.3 or 266
Antichrist	236
Antiquities	220.93
Apocrypha	229
Apologetics	239
Apostles	220.92
Apostles' Creed	238
Arabs and Jews	261.87
Archeology	220.93
Architecture, Church	254.7
Armageddon	226
Art and Christianity	261.5
Art, Religious	261.5
Arts and Crafts	268.474
Asia, Missions in	266.31
Astrology	290.2
Astronomy	261.5
Atheism	290.3
Athletics	268.477
Atlases	220.9
Atomic Bomb	261.87
Atonement	232.4
Audio/Visuals	268.42 or 254.3
Australia, Missions in	266.37
Authority, Bible	220.1
Authority, Church	262.9
Authorship, Bible	220.14
Autobiographies	267.1-4

B

Bahaism	290
Baptism	265
Beatitudes	226.93
Beauty	248.4
Beginner Child	268.4323

Beginner Department	268.4323
Behavior	268.478
Belief	234
Bereaved, Activities for	259.6
Bereaved, Ministry to	248.41 or 253
Betrayal by Judas	232.9
Bible	220
Bible, Authority of	220.1
Bible, Inspiration of	220.13
Bible, Interpretation of	220.6
Bible, Law and Historical Books	222
Bible, New Testament	225
Bible, Old Testament	221
Bible, Origin of	220.1
Bible, Study of	220
Bible and Science	215
Bible Archeology	220.93
Bible Authorship	220.14
Bible Canon	220.12
Bible Catechisms	238
Bible Chronology	220.9
Bible Colleges and Universities	207.1
Bible Customs	220.9
Bible Dictionaries	220.3
Bible Encyclopedias	220.3
Bible Evidences	239
Bible Festivals	220.944
Bible Geography	220.9
Bible Handbooks	220.2
Bible History	220.9
Bible Introduction	220
Bible Lands in Bible Times	220.9
Bible Manuscripts	220.41
Bible Maps	220.9
Bible Men	220.92
Bible Miracles	226.7
Bible Natural History	213
Bible Plays and Pageants	268.476
Bible Prophecy	220.15
Bible Questions or Problems	220.71

Calvinism	230.044
Camping	268.477
Campus Crusade for Christ	267.9
Canon, Bible	220.12
Capital Punishment	261.8
Careers	248.83
Cartoons	268.477H
Catacombs	270
Catechisms	238
Catholic Theology	230.042
Catholicism	280
Central America, Missions in	266.36
Chalk Talks	268.41
Chaplains	261.7
Character-Building Stories for Children	C
Charismatic Experience and Practice	248.29
Charismatic Movement	270
Charts	268.41 or 220.9
Chemistry	261.5
Child Abuse	261.831
Child Study	268.401
Child Training (Home)	248.432
Children, Exceptional	248.433 or 268.402
Children, Handicapped	248.433 or 268.402
Children in Other Lands	266
Children's Church	268.432
Children's Clubs	268.473
Children's Day	268.423
Children's Division, Christian Education	268.432
Children's Fiction	Fc
Children's Sermons	268.4326
Children's Songs	268.432
Choirs	264.2
Choral Speaking	264
Christ, Life of	232

Conversion	234 or 253.7
Conviction	234
Convicts	261.833
Cookbooks	248.846
Cookery	268.477 or 248.846
Corinthians, First	227.2
Corinthians, Second	227.3
Correspondence Schools and Courses	268.434
Costumes	268.475
Counseling	253.5
Courtesy	268.478
Courtship	248.42 or 248.83
Cradle Roll	268.4321
Crafts	268.474
Creation	213 or 231.765
Creation of Man	233
Creeds	238
Crime and Criminals	261.833
Criticism, Biblical	220.6
Cross	232.4
Crossword Puzzles	268.477
Crucifixion	232.4
Cults	290.2
Current Events	261.1 or 261.87
Curriculum, Church School	268.6
Curriculum, Sunday School	268.6
Customs, Bible	220.9

D

Daily Devotional Readings	242.2
Daily Vacation Bible school	268.471
Daniel	224.5
Darwinism	213
Dating	248.83
Deacons, Deaconesses	254
Dead Sea Scrolls	220.41
Death	236.1 or 248.41
Deity of Christ	232.8

Delinquency, Juvenile	261.83
Delinquents	261.833
Delivery, Sermon or Speech	251.03
Deluge	220.93
Democracy	261.7
Demonology	290.2
Demons	235.4
Denominations and Sects	280 or 250
Deuteronomy	222.15
Devil	235.4
Devotionals	242.2
Devotionals, Women's Society	245.2
Devotions, Family	242.23
Devotions for Adults	242.2
Devotions for Children	242.1
Devotions for Homemakers	242.21
Devotions for Men	242.21
Devotions for Nurses	242.21
Devotions for Pre-teens (Juniors)	242.101
Devotions for Teachers	242.21
Devotions for Young Teens	242.11
Devotions for Youth	242.12
Dictionaries, Bible	220.3
Dictionaries, General	030
Dictionaries, New Testament	225.3
Dieting	248.845
Disciples, Twelve	220.92
Discipleship	248.4
Discipline, Church	262.9
Discipling	248.5 or 253.7
Dispensations	230.044
Divine Healing	234.13 or 265
Divorce	248.421
Doctrine, Christian	230
Doctrine, Protestant (All Varieties)	230.044
Doctrines of Specific Denominations or Sects	230.1
Drama	268.475 or 268.476
Drug Abuse or Addiction	261.83

Evil Spirits   235.4
Evolution   213 or 239
Exceptional Child, Education of   268.402
Exceptional Child in the Home   248.433
Existentialism   290.3
Exodus   222.12
Exorcism   234.13 or 265
Extension Department   268.435
Ezekiel   224.4
Ezra   222.7

F
Faith (For Salvation)   234
Faith (Theological Study)   241.4
Faith in the Chri ...r Life   248.4
Faith Cure   234.13 or 265
Fall of Man   233
Family   246
Family Altar or Worship   248.43 or 242.23
Family of Jesus   232.9
Family Planning   248.43
Famine   261.86
Fascism   290.3
Fasting   248.845
Fasting, Biblical   220.944
Fathers   248.432
Father's Day   263
Fear   248.4
Feasts, Biblical   220.944
Festivals, Biblical   220.944
Fiction for Adults   F
Fiction for Children   Fc
Fiction for Juniors   J
Fiction for Young Teens   T
Fiction for Youth   Y
Filmstrips   268.41
Finance, Personal   248.412
Finances, Church   254.8
Financial Management   248.412
First Aid   248.845

Flags	268.479
Flood	220.93
Flowers, Biblical	220.8
Foreign Christian Literature	O (plus appropriate classification)
Foreign Language Bibles	220.53 or O-220.53
Foreign Missions	266.3
Forgiveness	234 or 248.4
Fortune-Telling	290.2
Fourth of July	263.91
France, Missions in	266.33
Free Will of Man	234.9
Freedom of Worship	261.72
Freedom, Religious	261.72
Fund Raising	254.8
Fundamentalism	230.044
Funerals, Christian	265
Furnishings, Christian Education or Sunday School	268.2
Furnishings, Church	254.7
Future Life	236
Future Punishment	236.9

G

Galatians	227.4
Games, Bible	220.8
Games, Social	268.477
Genesis	222.11
Geography, Bible	220.9
Geography, New Testament	225.09
Geology	261.5
Germany, Missions in	266.33
Gerontology	248.85
Gifts, Spiritual	234.13
Gifts of the Holy Spirit	231.22
Girl Scouts	268.473
Girls' Clubs	268.473
Globes	268.41

Glossolalia	248.29 or 234.13
God	231
God the Father	231.1
God the Holy Spirit	231.3
God the Son	231.2
Golden Rule	241.54
Good and Evil	230.044
Goodness of God	231
Gospels and Acts	226
Government and the Church	261.7
Grace	234
Graduation, Christian Education	268.423
Greek Language and Studies	220.41
Greek, New Testament	220.41
Grief	284.41
Grooming	248.842-3
Guidance, God's	234.12 or 248.4

H

Habakkuk	224.95
Handicapped, Activities for and with	259.4
Handicapped, Teaching the	268.402
Handicapped Child	248.433
Handicraft	268.474
Haggai	224.97
Happiness	248.4
Harmonies of Gospels	226.1
Healing, Divine	234.13 or 265.8
Health	248.845
Heathenism	266
Heaven	236.24
Hebrew Texts and Studies	220.4
Hebrew, Old Testament	220.4
Hebrews	227.87
Hell	236.25
Heresies	230
Hermeneutics (Bible Interpretation)	220.6
High School Department	268.4332
High School Youth	268.4332

John	226.5
John, First	227.94
John, Second	227.95
John, Third	227.96
Jokes	H
Jonah	224,92
Joshua	222.2
Judaism	290.1
Jude	227.97
Judges	222.32
Judgment	236.9
Judgment Day	236.9
Junior Child	268.4325
Junior Department	268.4325
Junior Fiction	J
Junior High Department	268.4331
Junior High Young Person	268.4331
Justice of God	231
Justification	234
Juvenile Delinquency	261.833

K

Kindergarten Children	268.4323
Kindergarten Department	268.4323
Kingdom of God	231.72
Kings, First	222.53
Kings, Second	222.54
Korea, Missions in	266.31

L

Labor and Christianity	261.1
Lamentations	224.3
Large-Print Books	L (plus regular classification)
Latter Day Saints	290
Last Things (Eschatology)	237
Law, Bible Books of	222
Law, Church	262.9
Laws, Biblical	220.944
Lay Leadership	254.51

Media	254.3
Medical Missions	266.025
Medicine and Christianity	265.1
Meditation	248.23
Meditations for Time of Illness, Trouble, and Bereavement	242.4
Membership, Church	254.5
Memorial Day	263.91
Men of the Bible	220.92
Mental Health	253.5
Messiah	232.1
Metaphysics	290.2
Micah	224.93
Microfilms	268.41 or 254.3
Migrant Labor	261.1
Military Service	261.87
Millennium	236
Minister, Life and Person	253.2
Ministerial Duties	253
Minister's Wife	253.2
Ministry	253
Ministry to the Bereaved or Ill	248.41 or 265
Ministry to and with Senior Citizens	259
Minor Prophets	224.9
Minorities and the Church	261.1
Miracles	231.73
Miracles, Bible	226.7
Missionary Education	266
Missionary Organizations	266
Missionary Stories	266.09
Missions, Foreign	266.023
Missions, Home	266.022
Missions, Medical	266.025
Missions in Africa	266.0232
Missions in Asia	266.0231
Missions in Central America	266.0236
Missions in Europe	266.0233
Missions in Miscellaneous Countries	266.0237

Missions in North America	266.0235
Missions in South America	266.0234
Mixed Marriage	248.422
Modernism	230.044
Mohammedanism	290
Money Management	248.412
Moral Issues	241.6
Morality	261.6 or 240
Morals	240
Mormonism	290
Moslemism	290
Mothers	248.432
Mother's Day	263
Motion Pictures	254.3 or 268.42
Movies, Use of	268.42 or 254.3
Music, Bible	220.8
Music, Church	264.2
Music, Rock	261.83
Musical Instruments	264
Musical Instruments, Biblical	220.8
Muslemism	290

N

Nahum	224.94
Names, Meaning of	248.43
Names of God	231
Narcotics	261.83
National Association of Evangelicals	280
National Council of Churches	280
National Sunday School Association	268
Nativity	232.9
Nature Study	268.479
Negroes	261.1
Nehemiah	222.8
New Birth	234
New Morality	261.83
New Testament Chronology	225.09
New Testament Introduction	225.1

New Year's Eve or Day	263.91
North America, Missions in	266.35
Nuclear Activity	261.87
Numerology, Bible	220.944
Numbers	222.14
Nursery	268.4322
Nutrition	248.845

O

Obadiah	224.91
Obedience	234 or 248.4
Object Lessons	268.421
Occultism	290.2
Occupations	248.83
Old Age	248.85
Old Testament Chronology	221.62
Old Testament Geography	221.62
Old Testament History	221.62
Old Testament Introduction	221
Orchestral Music	264
Ordinances, Church	265
Ordination of Women	262.1
Organ Music	264
Organization, Church	254
Organizations, Church	254.6
Origin of Species	213
Original Texts	220.41
Orthodox Eastern Church	280
Outdoor Life	268.477
Outlines, Sermon	251.02

P

Pacifism	261.87
Paganism	290
Pageants	268.476
Pain	248.41 or 265
Palestine	220.9
Palestine, Missions in	266.37
Papacy	230.042
Parables	266.8

Poetry	242.9
Political Ethics	261.11
Politics and Christianity	261.7
Pollution	261.836
Poverty	261.86
Prayer	248.32
Prayer, Corporate	264
Prayer Meetings	254.6
Prayers, Collection of	242.8
Prayers for Times of Illness, Trouble, or Bereavement	242.4
Preachers	253.2
Preaching	251
Predestination	234.9
Priesthood	220.944
Primary Child	268.4324
Primary Department	268.4324
Primers	E
Problems, Bible	220.71
Professions	248.83
Programs (Seasonal and Other)	268.476
Prohibition	261.832
Projectors	268.42
Promotion, Christian Education	268.423
Prophecy	220.15
Prophecy, Gift of	234.13
Prophecy, Last Days	236
Prophets	220.92
Prophets, Book of	224
Prophets, Minor	224
Protestantism	280 or 250
Proverbs	223.7
Psalms	223.2
Psalters	264.21
Psychiatry	253.5 or 261.5
Psychology, Child	268.401
Psychology, Pastoral	253.5
Psychology and Christianity	261.5
Public Relations	254.4
Public Speaking	254.51

Religious Poetry	242.9
Remarriage	248.421
Repentance	234
Resurrection of Jesus	232.5
Resurrection of Man	236
Retirement	248.85
Retreats, Church	254.6
Revelation, Bible	220.13
Revelation, Book of	228
Revival	269
Riddles	268.477
Rock Music	261.83
Roman Catholic Church	250 or 230.042
Romans	227.1
Rules of Order	262.1
Russia, Missions in	266.33
Ruth	222.35

S

Sabbath	263
Sacraments	265
Sacred Art	261.5
Sacred Days	263
Sacred Music	264.2
Sacred Places	263
Sacrifice	232.4
Sacrifices, Bible	220.944
Saints	235 or 234
Salvation	234
Salvation Army	267.9
Samuel, First	222.43
Samuel, Second	222.44
Sanctification	234
Satan	235
School, Christian	268
School, Parochial	268
Science and the Bible	215 or 220.93
Scientology	290
Second Advent	236 or 232.6
Sects, Christian	280

Secularism	290.3
Segregation	261.8
Seminars	207.1
Senior Citizens	248.85
Sermon on the Mount	226.9 or 241.53
Sermon Delivery	251.03
Sermon Illustrations	251.04 or H
Sermon Outlines	251.02
Sermon Preparation	251.01
Sermons	252
Sermons for Children	268.4326
Seven Last Words (On the Cross)	232.9
Seventh Day, Observance of	263
Sex Education	248.435
Sexual Ethics	261.11
Shintoism	290
Shrines	263
Sick, Ministry to	248.41
Sin	233
Single Parenting	248.434
Singles	248.44
Sins	241.3
Skepticism	290.3
Skits	268.476
Slavery	261.8
Slides	268.41
Smoking	261.83
Social Action	261.1
Social Problems and Christianity	261.8
Social Sciences	265.1
Social Work	261.1
Socialism	290.3
Socials	268.477
Sociology	261.1
Son of God	231.2
Song of Solomon	223.9
Songbooks	264.21
Songs for Children	268.432
Songs for Youth	268.433
Songs Visualized	268.41

Sorcery	290.2
Sorrow	248.41
Soul	230.044
Soul Winning	248.5
South America, Missions in	266.34
Sovereignty of God	231
Speaking, Public	254.51
Speaking in Tongues	248.29 or 234.13
Spirit	230.044
Special Studies	220.944
Spirit, Holy	231.3
Spiritualism	290.3
Spiritual Beings	235
Spiritual Gifts	234.13
Spiritual Renewal	269
Sports	268.477
Stars	261.5
Starvation	261.86
Stewardship	248.412
Stories, Bible—for Children	B
Stories, Bible—for Youth and Adults	220.9505
Stories, Character-Building— for Children	C
Stories, Missionary	266.09
Story Telling	268.4
Studies on Old Testament	221.7
Success	248.411
Suffering	248.41
Suicide	261.83
Summer Camps	268.477
Sunday	263
Sunday School	268
Sunday School Administration and Organization	268.1
Sunday School Curricula	268.6
Sunday School Promotion	268
Sunday School Superintendent	268.1
Survey, Bible	220.2
Symbolism	264

GLOSSARY

Glossary

Accession List. List of materials in the exact order in which they are first received into the library, numbering each item in that chronological order. Purposes for this list are: 1. to have the receiving date, the donor or source, and the price of each item in the library 2. to know the number of items in your library; and 3. to know which are the newest items in your library. There should be a separate accession list for each type of material. (See the sample accession sheet in the Appendix.)

Accession Number. The number of each item in the order of its addition to the library. This number is not put on the outside of the book, and the book is not shelved by this number.

Book Pocket. The library pocket, pasted inside the back cover (or on the page facing the back cover) of each book, holds the borrower's card (book card) when the book is in the library. The pocket is also attached to other types of library materials when it is feasible to do so.

Borrower's Card (book card or pocket card). Printed identification card kept in the book pocket in each book and in such materials as will allow a pocket. With non-book items, when a pocket is not feasible, the borrower's card is usually kept in a borrower's file. When a borrower checks out an item, he writes on this card his name and the date on which the item is due back in the library. He leaves the card with the librarian so that she will have a record of who has the material and when it is due to be returned. During the time the material is out on loan, the borrower's card is filed in a date file.

Borrower's Card File. Narrow file (like the date file) used to keep borrowers' cards for types of materials which do not permit a borrower's card to be filed wth or on the material. These cards are filed alphabetically by title and are removed to a date file when the item is borrowed.

Cataloguing. The complete procedure of processing material for loan in the library.

Classification Number (or Call Number). Subject number of the individual item by which it is placed on the library shelves. (See the "Classification System" Section.)

Classification System. An arrangement of numbers which covers every subject to which a library item can relate. Each item in your church library comes under a subject heading for which there is a number in the classifying system in this manual. This number is to be printed on the back of each book cover or jacket or in an obvious place on other materials, and the material is shelved in this numerical order. The system in this manual is the Dewey Decimal system, very slightly adapted for more convenient church library use.

Classifying. The process of determining the subject number for each particular library item.

Date Due Slip. Slip (pasted on the page opposite the book pocket) for recording the date by which the book is due back in the library. When the borrower checks out a book, the due date (usually two weeks from the current date) is recorded as a reminder to him of the date by which the book should be returned to the library.

Date File or Charging Tray. Tall, narrow file, with 34 dividers (1-31 days of the month, "This month," "Next month" and "Overdue"), in which the borrower's cards are kept when materials are out of the library. Cards are filed in the date file according to their due date.

File Cards. (Work, Title, Author, Subject). These are 3 x 5 plain white or buff cards on which is typed key information for each item in the library.

Financial Record. Record in which all library money receipts and disbursements are recorded. (See sample sheet in the Appendix.)

Visuals and Audio/Visuals. Visuals are those items which are visuals only (no sound). Audio/visuals refer to items which are either audio (sound) or visual or both.

SAMPLE FORMS

DATE DUE			
GAYLORD			PRINTED IN U.S.A.

Sample date due slip

242	531
CLASS	ACC

Lew

Lewis, C. S.

(LAST NAME OF AUTHOR)

Screwtape Letters

(BOOK TITLE)

DATE DUE	ISSUED TO

242
Lew   531

Sample borrower's card and pocket

Sample Book Accession Sheet

DATE	ACCESSION NUMBER	AUTHOR	TITLE	PUBLISHER	YEAR	COST	REMARKS

Sample Audio/Visual Accession Sheet

DATE	ACCESSION NUMBER	Speaker/Artist	TITLE	PUBLISHER	YEAR	COST	REMARKS

Sample Financial Record

DATE	RECEIPTS	AMT.	DISBURSEMENTS	AMT.	BALANCE

APPENDIX

Shelf Tabs

000	General Works
200	Religion
220	Bible
221-224	Old Testament
225-228	New Testament
230-238	Doctrine

239	Apologetics
241	Christian Moral Theology
242	Devotional
248.2-248.41	Christian Life
248.42-248.9	Christian Marriage and Family
248.83	Youth Only
250-259	Christian Church
261.83-87	Social Problems
262-265	Church Observances
266	Missions

267.1-4	Biography
268	Christian Education
268.432	Children's Work
268.433	Youth Work
268.434	Adult Work
268.47	Activities
290	Other Religions
L	Large Print
F	Fiction for Youth and Adults
T	Fiction for Young Teens

J	Fiction for Juniors
Fc	Fiction for Children
B-C-E	Children's Stories
O	Foreign Language

Make a cardboard stencil from this pattern and use to pencil in top and bottom score lines on back edge of books.

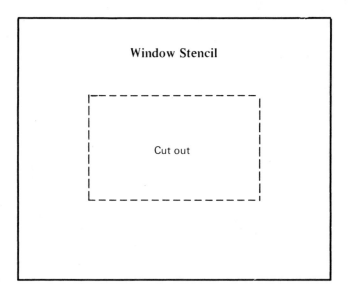

Window Stencil

Cut out

Window Stencil

How To Use Your Library

Your church library is a MINISTER of your church. Use it—with gratitude and respect!

If you do not find the material you want, refer to our card files or ask the librarian to help you.

When you have selected a book, sign the book card in the back cover pocket. Take the card and book to the librarian for checking out.

When you wish to borrow a non-book item, take the item to the librarian and allow her/him to locate the borrower's card for you to sign.

Treat the library material with consideration and care. Do not mark or turn down pages, or in any way deface an item.

Return material by the due date. Leave the item on the librarian's desk or other designated place. Please do not return it to the shelf.

Renew the item (once only) if you find it inconvenient to return it by the date due. You may phone or write your renewal.

Please pay overdue fees immediately and cheerfully.

Watch the bulletin board and posters for new material listings and suggestions.

Tell your friends about the church library and of the good helps you have found here.